KU-674-199

Minxy
VINTAGE

For Katie Bullen, who gave me cashmere,
and Olive: in absence of heirlooms of any real worth,
these are my treasures — they are yours to keep.

Minxy VINTAGE

How to Customise and Wear Vintage Clothing

KELLY DOUST

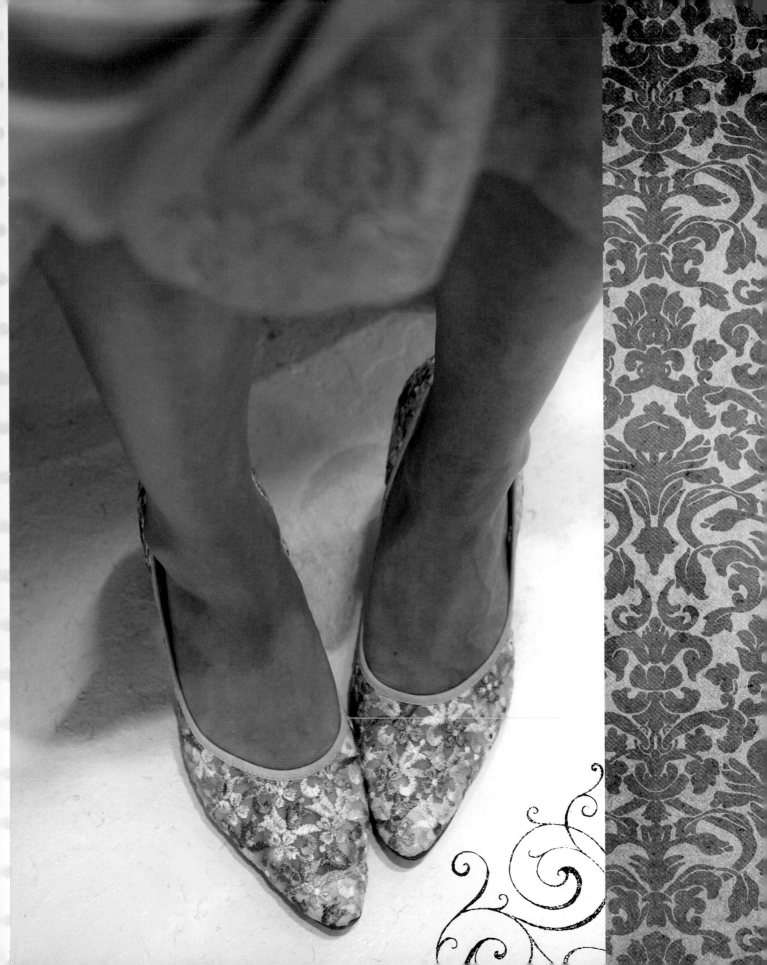

Foreword

ALONG WITH A PENCHANT FOR LAVISH HIGH tea parties and being the mothers of small children born a week apart, Kelly and I share a mutual love of vintage clothing. We met when she visited my vintage clothing boutique, Coco Repose, and have been friends ever since; a relationship forged over our mutual passion—and admiration for—the elegance of vintage style. It has been my great pleasure to share an insight into the creation of this lovely book, and provide Kelly with some of the garments you'll find here within Minxy Vintage.

As a vintage clothing dealer, I love nothing more than matching the perfect vintage piece with the thoroughly modern woman it deserves to go to, and giving it a second chance at life. All too frequently, I watch customers try on and look fantastic in a piece, but walk away because they don't have the confidence to forge a unique style of their own, or lack an understanding of how to wear an item so that it doesn't look out of place by today's standards.

While the pieces I sell haven't been altered to hold on to their integrity, there is a trick to wearing vintage in a modern way, which Kelly articulates and demonstrates through her own unique style—whether it be by pairing with contemporary accessories, making alterations to fit, or reinventing with a total makeover.

When you come upon special vintage finds, I encourage you to make them work for your body shape and lifestyle. Enjoy and recycle these works of art, which have already survived the test of time. There are only so many times a vintage piece can be 'rediscovered', and only so many vintage dresses in the world, but wouldn't the original owner be thrilled to know their favourite piece is being worn again to a friend's wedding, out to dinner on a date, or even to the races for fashions on the field, albeit in a new guise?

It is important to understand the eras your favourite pieces come from, and the history surrounding them. I particularly enjoy hearing the comments made by partners of women who wear vintage clothing. They frequently notice how alluring a dress is, even if they don't understand why, when vintage pieces are often dramatically more demure than today's fashion. This is because most clothes were custom-made, and designers worked incredibly hard to flatter a woman's figure, rather than adopting the one-size-fits-many approach of today. A fitted waistline can be just as sexy as a plunging v-neck: just look to some of those women from the past who were considered total bombshells, despite the lack of bare flesh on display.

Although there are so many books on the history of vintage clothing, I love that *Minxy Vintage* explains how to alter and wear pieces now. Maybe I shouldn't admit to this, but it always puts a smile on my face when others admire my favourite items—whether it be a summer dress, or a silk bed jacket worn with jeans. No matter how much they lust after it, they simply can't go out and buy the same one, because mine was made in 1953!

Enjoy the richness of fabric, the decadence in design, and history and art form unique to each item of vintage clothing. But most of all, enjoy the frivolity of dressing up each day. Step outside an industry of mass-manufacture, and create a unique style all of your own by mixing vintage pieces with your existing wardrobe. And discover just how easily an unusual hat or dress can completely change your look, and provide you with the confidence to be that person you always wanted to be.

Jessica Guthrie
Owner, Coco Repose

Contents

Contents

BOUDOIR BASICS AND SAUCY SHAPEWEAR   232

SOME LAST THOUGHTS ON STYLE   252

ACKNOWLEDGEMENTS   254

Reinventing
Vintage Fashion

'You can have everything you want in life if you dress for it.'
— Edith Head

Wearing vintage clothing is such an adventure. The history (and mystery) in older pieces can be as addictive as a drug. The pure drama of being able to slip in and out of different identities, and add new chapters to an item's story ... well, it's nothing less than a thrill. And it's never a great leap to imagine the fabulous host of soirees my clothes might have seen before they became mine. I also count myself lucky every day that, in the times we live in, anything goes—it's lovely not being restricted by a style when your body shape cries out for something else. Just imagine the agony of being a curvy fifties shape in the Roaring Twenties, when flat-chested figures were all the rage.

The possibility of owning incredibly well-made items—the likes of which cost a small fortune to produce nowadays, but can be bought for a song secondhand—is also irresistible to me. Indeed, many of the most treasured items in my wardrobe first found their way in there via flea markets, charity and vintage clothing stores, and I swear to feeling more affection for them than all but a few of the items I bought brand-spanking new and on-trend.

But this is not just a book about loving vintage fashion—it's about seeing the possibilities for reinventing it, and how to look fabulous doing so, no matter what your age or budget.

It takes a degree of self-awareness and personal style to wear vintage with conviction on a daily basis: although vintage trends come and go, it's far more difficult to navigate your way through the secondhand marketplace than it is to kit yourself out in the offerings from current designers. But that's the beauty of pulling together the old and the new: it's one of the best ways I know to ensure your style stays fresh, unique and individual.

One thing to keep in mind when you're fossicking through old clothes is that much of today's quality vintage clothing is yesterday's designer fashion. But although there's certainly a collectible element to buying vintage, I don't believe in treating clothes as delicate antiques—they are designed to be worn,

and worn out. Life's too short to be too precious, which is why I refuse to save my favourite things for so-called special occasions, preferring to wear them every day.

The purpose of this book is to introduce you to my vintage staples, and pass on simple ideas for wearing, customising and totally reinventing them to create a glamorous, high-fashion look for next to nix (the wardrobe equivalent of quaffing champagne on a beer budget). I'm all for blow-out shopping sprees once in a while, but the bottom line is, you don't need to spend a fortune to look a million bucks. This book is intended to give you the tools required to look through piles of seemingly disappointing cast-offs and assess them for their true potential.

When it comes to shopping for garments and accessories, there's something about the thrill of the hunt that hooks and mesmerises me—I love a challenge. Finding my latest fashion fix in a run-of-the-mill chainstore never inspires the same heady sense of satisfaction as alighting upon that perfect, precious find under a jumbled mountain of unsuitable items. And as I move closer towards the approximation of a grown-up, I find that I move further away from the youthful tendency to want to look like everybody else. This is why regular high-street stores are somewhat ruined for me, with their limited stock and necessarily trend-dictated approach.

Wearing items from every era will give any wardrobe a timeless edge, and will date it far less quickly than investing in the latest season's fashions. Particularly if you don't go overboard and wear head-to-toe vintage, choosing to pair old pieces with new instead. When done properly, this looks fresh and modern (indeed, stylists and designers do it all the time). It also injects your style with real personality. And as I've never turned up to a party wearing the same outfit as somebody else, I can honestly say it's a practice that works for me. Of course I've had sartorial hits and misses—haven't we all? But oh, I've had some fun in the process! And as old blue eyes sang: *I did it my way*.

In the nineties, when I was a teen, I was no different from the rest of my generation. It was the time for trawling secondhand stores looking for clothes we fancied made us look like seventies rock stars—fully paid-up subscribers to the grunge movement, which originated in America's Seattle. We were desperate to get our hands on that most prized of items, a distressed flannelette shirt, but I also remember a particular fondness for faded Levi's 501 jeans, Chinese embroidered silk blouses worn elegantly dishevelled, Swedish clogs, wraparound Thai fisherman's trousers, A-line mini dresses and flowing cotton kaftans, layered under strings of beads and clanking bangles worn halfway up the arm; always paired with a large pair of sunnies (and a peace sign somewhere or other) and always, preferably, pre-loved. The universality of these items gives you an indication of the possibilities of vintage items, and the personalities we are able to take on when we wear them.

During that recession, which saw my job prospects dwindle and further study seem the only available option, fossicking for thrifty pieces to furnish my personal style was born out of necessity and commonsense. But long after the trend and need subsided, I held on to my fascination for vintage shopping and continued to devote a large proportion of my spare time to discovering something new to love in other people's junk.

It's become a major element of my lifestyle, and a way in which I define myself today. And just as the nature of fashion is circular, its popularity has come around. Recycling clothes is my passion, and I've done it for as long as I can remember. From when I first had my own money coming in at the age of twelve—earned through a glamorous job cleaning buckets at a local florist—up to yesterday, when I found a pure-wool Sonia Rykiel mini tube skirt in a flea market, in this season's most covetable shade. The label boasts its collection date: 1989. With its recent coming-of-age, it has proved itself a lasting companion. I wouldn't be surprised if it becomes a lifelong friend.

For me, clothes are not merely inanimate objects, but companions of every variety to share the journey with. From the old staples who've seen me through tough times, to the fair-weather types who only flatter me when I'm at my best, to new lovers who seduce from across the room, when spied upon a crowded rack … And just like all the friends I've had over the years, I cherish each and every one of them for their unique charms.

As so many of us are in times of relative affluence, I'm a terribly willing consumer, buying new things for my wardrobe and household. But they're not often new, just new for me, and don't need to be unworn to give me that kick from stepping out in a frock for the first time.

There's no denying that vintage clothes require maintenance, but I've always thought there is real beauty in the threadbare and love-worn. I long to see the evidence of a rich history, both in my clothes and in my people. In details like the scuffs on a pair of cowboy boots, say, or fade lines on my jeans … overly washed cottons and crushed silks are deliciously beautiful, too, both to look at and wear. In contrast, brand new clothes can be the same as a very young face: desirable for its pristine beauty, but without much character—a depth which only comes through a good many years of living and experience.

My clothes cost little, so I'm not only not restricted by my modest budget, I'm also not overly worried about damaging them, or having to think how dreadfully expensive they are every time I wear them.

But the most wonderful element of appreciating this pre-loved fashion is that, when I'm done, I pass favourite pieces I've become bored with on to friends, or to strangers, by holding my own market stall. Or I donate them to my local charity store. I've no qualms about loving and leaving clothes—the way they pass through our lives is entirely natural, as long as it's done without carelessness. Buying quality items or altering inexpensive pieces to make them more wearable means they not only stand the test of time, but do us proud in the interim.

As an ardent lover of vintage, I can attest to the importance of finding clothes you can integrate into your existing style. I'm not about stridently holding up the ideals of other eras—the modern world is grand. It's precisely the mix of old and new that I love. Wearing a natty number from the forties paired with a mussed-up 'do and plaited leather friendship bands can be so much more chic than setting your hair and wearing patent pumps to match. And who wants to be, or slavishly replicate, a woman in the pre-feminist 1940s? Certainly not me. Go gaga over slinky silk slips but add a pair of biker boots and a cropped leather jacket instead of the diamanté clasps and strappy sandals. Clash masculine and feminine, soft and hard, loose and fitted silhouettes, old and new, and be brave with colour and pattern—at least once in a while. Play with preconceptions to avoid being a victim, or a slave, to the latest trends. It's the way to stand out, in a good way.

Long live fashion—where would we be without you?—and long last its thrilling irreverence, relevance and capacity for injecting such fun into our lives. Long live our love for cherry-picking the best bits from the past, and making them new again: reinvention, rather than nostalgia. Whatever you do, just make sure you own it. Individuality is a quality to be admired.

Vintage threads, I sincerely heart you.

Kelly

15€

For the aristocratic French family laes →tam

Getting
STARTED

OVER THE YEARS I'VE BEEN ASKED BY FRIENDS TO TAKE them along on my shopping jaunts to markets, auction houses, charity stores, vintage clothing emporiums and fabric shops, acting as a kind of personal shopper to help them find the perfect outfit for a special occasion. Sometimes, I've even helped them look for a whole new wardrobe. I don't know if I could do it for a stranger—it's so much easier with a friend because I can be honest about what I think, and they trust me. It helps to be familiar with someone's personal style and the fashion rules they've set themselves, before urging them to try something new. Otherwise it's all about pushing my own sense of style onto them, rather than encouraging them to develop their own.

Areas of resistance I've had to overcome during these trips are others' aversion to musty old things—*dead people's clothes,* as one friend referred to them—and expensive tastes. Some of my friends simply have an unrelenting fondness for designer items. The first I counteract with cleaning, and the enigmatic adventures of its former occupant, taking them on a romantic journey of the imagination to inject the humble piece in their hands with some glamour beyond the grave, as it were. The second is easier: it isn't hard to work out that many of today's pre-loved items are yesterday's couture; the most well-designed items were made to last—you just need to know how to spot them. I suffer from the almost polar opposite affliction to my friends: it's nigh on impossible for me to part with, say, five hundred dollars for a new frock without thinking: *But remember the time I found that stack of pristine silk 1960s Japanese kimonos for several dollars each, and turned one into a fabulous party frock?*

But by far the most difficult issue I have to counteract is an inability to see beyond the item to its wonderful possibilities for reinvention. As my friend Colette says, she can spend hours flicking through the items in a secondhand market or store, unable to find anything appropriate, when someone else will come along and pull out a stunning item before heading to the counter … while she stands there wondering how on earth she could have overlooked it! It is my wish that, in reading this book, you'll learn to identify the pieces worth reinventing even when they appear, at first glance, uninspiring.

My number-one favourite place to find vintage clothing is at flea markets, but car-boot sales, garage sales, deceased estates and auction houses can also be a treasure trove of forgotten pieces—just be careful not to get too carried away when you're bidding at auction. If you don't trust yourself to stick to your budget, most auction houses will allow you to leave an absentee bid, or ring you when a favoured item comes up so you can bid over the phone. And remember to factor in the auctioneers' commission, on top of your final bid. It's also likely the piece you want will be included in a job lot, along with other items, so be prepared to purchase things you won't necessarily be interested in.

If I have time on my hands and am in the mood for a rummage, I will hunt for real bargains at my local flea market. On these occasions, I tend to veer towards the one-off or irregular sellers (rather than the weekly stall holders); women like me, who are clearing out their closets to go travelling or because they're sick of working a certain look—they're there to have a bit of fun and make some spare cash, and want to sell everything they came with

rather than taking anything back home. Be prepared to put in the time looking, though, because these items are unlikely to be edited down to the best pieces, or displayed nicely.

That said, forming a good relationship with a regular stall holder or the owner of a vintage clothing store can be a wonderful boon: some will give you a call when they find an item in your size or style, and will place it aside if you ask them. Just be aware you're paying a premium for their expertise and overheads. But they will have a better-edited collection, so you won't need to spend as much time sorting through rubbish (and by that I mean cheap, badly made, mass-produced chainstore pieces).

Another spot for vintage bargains is in charity stores. Certain areas are better than others: wealthy suburbs often boast fabulously well-stocked charity stores with a plethora of secondhand designer pieces, because that's where the locals dump their cast-offs after a good spring clean. Consignment stores are also a source of pre-loved designer fashion, if labels are your thing. This is where women take their unwanted clothes from the previous few seasons, often splitting the item's price fifty-fifty with the owner of the store. If you're tempted to buy brand-new designer clothes or accessories, have a hunt through a consignment store first before hitting Net-a-Porter, the department stores and boutiques. They're not super-cheap, but will save you at least half off the original retail price, and sometimes far more.

Designer vintage stores are becoming more and more popular, particularly in the big international cities. New York, London and Paris have many to choose from—the most renowned being places such as Didier Ludot in Paris and Decades in Los Angeles. I love the vintage clothing concession at London's Liberty department store, which boasts a heady collection of vintage Chanel, Yves Saint Laurent, Mary Quant and Dior. This is where you'll find stylists hunting for something rare and original to clothe their clients in for the red carpet. The Corner Shop in Sydney also has a small selection of designer vintage pieces.

In designer vintage stores, the quality is superb and racks well-edited, but the items are still usually beyond my budget. I also find it hard to fork out for designer vintage when I've had so much success in flea markets with both designer and no-name vintage pieces. I do own vintage designer items, such as the black eighties woollen Yves Saint Laurent dress I found in a flea market for next to nothing, but by far my most cherished pieces are those exquisitely handmade items from the forties, fifties and sixties, which were copied from designs by the major Parisian couture houses. No less beautiful for their humble provenance, they were likely overlooked because they didn't have a flashy label.

And there's always eBay. I'm too nervous about ordering clothes online (once bitten, twice shy … I've had a few disasters with sizing and mounting postage costs) and I miss the tactile element when I'm online shopping, but many friends have success stories about shopping for vintage online. Even I've done well in the area of accessories. Many of the sellers provide detailed information on sizing, flagging any issues such as marks or damage. But don't let my reticence stop you: if I lived in the countryside or didn't travel overseas every once in a while, I'm sure that hopping online would be one of my favourite ways to shop for vintage.

What to look for

HOW TO MINE FOR VINTAGE GOLD AMONGST ALL THE JUNK? Easy. Just follow the guiding factors below. None is a hard and fast rule, but all should help you discern whether something is worth investing the time and money in.

LUXE FABRICS

Silk, heavy satin, velvet, leather, linen and 100 percent wool or cotton. Don't be afraid to get up close and personal—rub material between your fingertips; how does it feel? Could you wear it comfortably against your skin? Quality fabrics are used for quality garments, on the whole, so this is your first and best hint that you're in the presence of vintage royalty. Well-respected designers do use man-made materials in the interests of durability, or for spectacular effect (I love a bit of lamé, for example) but, for my money, natural fibres are the way to go. Well-designed textiles such as crepe, jersey (which falls so beautifully) and glimmering brocades are also well worth collecting. Weigh up the item in your hands: if it's heavy, it's worth a good once-over. It is my experience that many of the best frocks from earlier eras have a pleasing weight to them.

ELEGANT DETAILS

Consider things such as hanging straps, lining, interfacing, well-hidden zips and those clever press-stud clips that hold your bra straps in place on a top or frock. Look out for luxurious buttons and beading, or a tag that says 'dry clean only', or detailed washing instructions paired with quality fabric. Pattern matching (when the design on the fabric is matched at the seams, so the garment looks almost seamless) is also a giveaway for masterful design. These little extras are expensive for manufacturers to add to their clothes during production; the waste involved in pattern-matching is huge, for example, so it's usually carried out on only the very best pieces. If the garment is cheap (what I would call 'throwaway' fashion), it probably won't include these thoughtful elements.

SIGNS OF ITS ERA

There are a few clever ways to tell the age of an item, even when the label is missing. The general guide to stick to, classification-wise, is this: anything made prior to the 1920s is antique, the twenties to sixties era is true vintage, and the seventies to eighties era clothes are actually more what you'd call 'retro'. At this stage, anything from the nineties onwards is just secondhand. Prior to the 1940s, zippers were not used on anything other than uniforms; designers opted for press-studs and elasticated waists to do the job of fitted tailoring instead. A decade later, metal zippers became popular in frocks and skirts, but were fitted along the side of a garment and often under the arm. In the 1950s, designers worked out it was easier to have a long metal zip down the spine rather than along its side, so dresses of the era often feature zippers here. The nylon zipper was invented in the 1960s, so anything with a nylon zipper could only have been created after this time (unless the zipper has been replaced at a later date; look closely for evidence of this).

And in the 1970s the overlocker was widely used, which means you can be fairly sure anything with overlocked seams is from the 1970s or later. It's common to confuse some 1980s dresses with the 1950s, because the trend for fifties styling came back into fashion then. But if it has a nylon zip *and* overlocking, you know it's definitely from the 1980s or later.

GRAND AND ONCE-GRAND DESIGNS

Designers make mistakes, too, but if you swot up on your fashion history, present and future, you're far more likely to spot the real bargains when hunting for pre-loved things. Pretty much everything I've learned about fashion I've read in *Vogue*. I also spend hours flicking through the fashion sections of bookstores and libraries, and go gaga over fabulous fashion blogs and the 'new in store' section at Net-a-Porter (which I visit religiously, referencing it as a form of online magazine for the very latest fashions). Keep in mind, though, that a designer label counts for nought if the item's not well-made.

Top tips for vintage shopping

TRY EVERYTHING ON

That means *everything*, from the cheapest T-shirt pulled out of the two-dollar box to the best designer frock you've ever come across in a vintage boutique. I customise almost every secondhand item I buy, but it still needs to be halfway there in terms of fit or colour or fabric, and if it's damaged I'll come up with a crafty solution to fixing it *before* I fork out money. Sometimes there's only so much surgery you can do; if the job is too ambitious, it's highly likely you'll never get around to it. Trying items on is also the very best way to figure out the shapes that suit you, and those that don't. It helps you develop an eye for what works for your figure, even when the item's hanging on the rack, and keeps your wardrobe free of things you'll never wear. (One trick: if you're not sure whether the waistline will fit you, wrap the waist around your neck; if both sides meet at the back, it should do.)

WORK OUT WHAT YOU LIKE

Always have those items running through your head when you're rifling through things. My list is *long,* and I'm always on the lookout for any of the following: evening dresses from the 1920s, 1930s and 1950s, sixties shifts and Wiggle dresses, beaded cashmere cardigans and quirky boleros, eighties cocktail frocks, seventies kaftans, snakeskin clutches, delicate beaded evening purses, sixties and seventies high-heeled dancing boots, peep-toe shoes, cowboy boots, elastic-waisted belts from the 1980s, low-slung leather belts from the 1970s, cocktail hats, felt hats, cute brooches and cameos, cuffs and bangles from any era in wood or gold-plate, and Chinois-style silk tops and cheongsams. If I had to pick a favourite era, I'd probably say the seventies for relaxed, ethnic-inspired charm by day, and fifties by night for its dramatic glamour—but I dip in and out of various styles from the previous century on a daily basis. I'm even partial to a bit of prim Victoriana every once in a while—thank goodness Vivienne Westwood revived the peplum and bustle, in a way we modern women can wear!

BE PATIENT

The best bargains aren't always going to offer themselves up to you. Vintage shopping has become a competitive sport these days; if you're not willing to roll your sleeves up and hunt through that bargain basket, or engage your imagination, you're never going to find those pieces some other shopper has overlooked.

LOOK FAR AFIELD

If, like me, you live in an inner-city environment (particularly one located near a university or full of fashionable people), you'll know that truly bargain vintage finds are few and far between. Try visiting charity shops and flea markets in country towns, or those located in the outer suburbs of your area. I hit the mother lode once when accompanying a surfer friend to the beach at Lorne, a couple of hours west of Melbourne. While he caught the waves, I went for a coffee and roamed the one short shopping strip, coming upon the town's sole charity store. In the window was a pair of strappy silver sandals from the 1970s, barely worn. When I inquired inside as to their size and price (a perfect fit and a few dollars for the pair), the shop assistant told me they'd been donated—along with thirty other pairs, many in their original designer boxes and dating from the 1950s to the 1980s— by a woman who had just moved her mother to a nursing home. I bought ten pairs (one Christian Dior, another Bruno Magli, and the others from various other designers) and wore them to death over the next five years. One pair, from closed-down Melbourne department store, Georges, still survives in my collection nearly twenty years on. They're a pair of 1960s-fabulous snakeskin pumps with a silver heel and buckle. The memory of that day still makes me smile.

BARGAIN

If the item is out of your price range, don't be afraid to bargain or ask if they offer a lay-by service—in flea markets bargaining is almost expected, but don't be disrespectful: there's no need to point out all the flaws in an item or be rude to the stallholder. It's all in the way you ask, so be nice. And don't make them a ridiculous offer. I bargain when I genuinely think something is too expensive or beyond my budget, and I always do it with a smile on my dial. If someone likes you on the spot, they'll often find a way for you to buy it. I know this to be true because whenever I've held my own market stalls to get rid of the clutter in my wardrobe, I'm more amenable to friendly, polite people who aren't grabby or rude. (That said, I hate it when someone tries bargaining an item down in a charity store, no matter how nicely it's done. If it's really too expensive in that environment, just walk away.)

Useful equipment

I'm a firm advocate of starting small when it comes to buying sewing equipment, rather than stocking up on a whole bunch of things I might not use. There's simply no need to go out and blow a small fortune in one fell swoop—finding out what you like, and what works best, takes time. Up until halfway through writing this book, I was still using the secondhand sewing machine I bought, along with its manual, from a flea market. Like an old, beloved car she had a few quirks, but saw me through the past seven years and the writing of two craft books with little more than broken needles. That was, until she started chewing up fabric in her old age … I bit the bullet and bought a modest new one on sale. I still plan to have the old one fixed one day and so keep it, just in case.

To begin with, all you really need to purchase are some hand needles and thread, plus a top-notch pair of dressmaking scissors. As with a chef's knife, go for the best you can afford: this is one item to truly splash out on because, with proper care, you'll reap the dividends of durability over the course of a lifetime.

And when you start getting serious about reinventing almost everything you buy, consider buying a dressmaker's dummy for tailoring jobs. Again, halfway through writing this book, I grew tired of getting undressed every five minutes to try something on and check if I'd tailored it correctly. I bought a dummy with adjustable measurements, which I've set to my size. She now dutifully stands in the corner of the room, waiting to be frocked or de-frocked several times a day. I'll also be able to use her to tailor things for friends, so I know the investment will pay off.

FINDING OUT WHAT YOU LIKE, AND WHAT WORKS BEST, TAKES TIME

Here are some of the items I find most useful, but I certainly wouldn't suggest you head out tomorrow and buy them all at once:

- a tape measure
- bobble-headed pins
- fine sewing needles
- a thimble (if you are a little clumsy like me and tend to prick yourself)
- large embroidery/tapestry needles
- the aforementioned dressmaking scissors
- small, sharp scissors for loose threads— I love my golden bird ones … so sweet
- pinking shears (scissors with a zig-zag edge: good for cutting fabrics that fray, such as canvas or linen)
- dressmaker's chalk
- Quick Unpick/seam ripper
- a sewing machine
- standard machine needles
- denim machine needles
- machine needles for delicate fabrics, such as silk or organza
- bobbins and a bobbin case
- sidewinder (this is a separate bobbin winder—you can wind bobbins on your machine, so you don't really need it, but they come in handy when you're using your machine a lot)
- a dressmaker's dummy (for the seriously crafty).

Additional fancy fripperies

Customising clothes is not as much fun unless you experiment with all the little extras you can buy to add flair and individuality to each piece. Buy threads in a rainbow of luscious hues for delectable contrasts, as well as ribbons, buttons, beads and sequins galore. Often quite cheap (or certainly affordable), these are the items to snap up when you see them, or else you might find yourself regretting it later, and going back to find they've disappeared. Buy a few of the following items here and there, and before you know it you'll have a delicious selection of things to choose from when it comes to 'upcycling' that one special item.

- A selection of threads—black, white, beige and navy are the basics, but it's good to build up a whole rainbow of colours for use on all fabrics. The general rule is to match thread to your fabric (cotton for cotton, silk for silk and polyester or cotton for synthetics), but cotton-polyester threads are sturdy and work well on most fabrics. Colour-wise, anything goes: use a contrasting colour if you want to highlight hems, or a shade darker than your fabric if you want it to blend in. A good tip is to wind half of your bobbins with basic colours at the same time, so they're ready when you need them
- embroidery thread, also in a range of colours— red, white, black, hot pink and electric blue are a great start for lovely contrasts
- balls of wool in colours you adore
- fabrics of every colour, pattern, texture and weave under the sun
- wool felt in candy colours
- calico

BUY THREADS IN A RAINBOW OF LUSCIOUS HUES FOR DELECTABLE CONTRASTS, AS WELL AS RIBBONS, BUTTONS, BEADS AND SEQUINS

- ribbons—grosgrain and velvet are my particular favourites
- buttons—I buy mine at flea markets and charity stores, because new buttons are so pricey. But eBay is also great for vintage numbers in shell, horn, ivory, wood, ceramic or Bakelite
- rickrack
- feathers
- sequins
- beads
- bias-binding, especially the thicker kind— these days you can find a gorgeous selection decorated with stripes, polka dots and cabbage rose-style florals
- interfacing
- broken jewellery—put aside any old jewellery or broken earrings and necklaces you might have. You never know when they could be useful for adorning an item of clothing
- pretty scraps of fabric, even if they are tiny and slightly trashed: silk, velvet and floral prints are great as a luxe patch when a moth hole or tear appears in an otherwise-perfect item of apparel.

SNAP UP GORGEOUS BOLTS
OF FABRIC, EMBROIDERY AND
TAPESTRY WHENEVER YOU SEE
THEM—EVEN SMALL PIECES
CAN BE RE-PURPOSED

CRAFTY REPAIRS
An Overview

A WHILE BACK, MY PARENTS-IN-LAW WANTED TO BUY MY husband and me a gift. At the time, our washing machine was on the blink and in the habit of erratically shredding our clothes. When my beloved pair of pyjama pants—in a fine, floral-sprigged cotton—ripped apart at the seams after a particularly violent cycle, I thought, enough's enough, and we requested they buy us a fancy new washing machine instead of the camera they had suggested. Not glamorous, I know, but we were desperate—the camera could wait.

I feel like a 1950s housewife admitting it, but that washing machine's changed my life. I've gone from spending, on some occasions, two hours handwashing my delicate silk and cashmere numbers each week, to entrusting them to our new washer's delicate or wool cycles. And that's the point of technology, don't you think? Imagine what it was like hundreds of years ago, before the invention of the household washing machine; women must have spent a great proportion of their lives washing clothes … No wonder there wasn't a feminist revolution until the 1960s—who had the time?

I avoid dry-cleaning as much as possible. All those chemicals are hell on the environment, and I've decided they don't always do such a brilliant job at removing stains or lingering perspiration smells. You're far better off buying customised, environmentally friendly cleaning products for your clothes, such as wool washes (I use them for wool *and* silk); surfactant-based stain removers (such as Sard Wonder Soap) which are unbeatable for removing all sorts of things; soaking agents for whites; starch or spray for ironing; and eucalyptus or tea-tree oil for removing oil marks or sticky things such as chewing gum. And who can forget a trusty bottle of white wine vinegar for killing musty mould and perspiration smells dead, a few drops of lavender oil for a sweet scent refresh, or baking soda for particularly stubborn stains.

If you don't have a wonderful new machine and you *do* have a wardrobe full of vintage clothes and delicates, try ditching the dry-cleaning for a careful handwash in the bath, agitating the water as little as possible, and gently pressing the excess liquid from the fibres before laying items flat to dry (rather than wringing them).

If it's the dry-cleaning 'finish' you're after, how about taking your clothes to the dry-cleaners for a professional press? I do it all the time, as I *loathe* ironing more than almost any other household chore, and one should never underestimate how a good press can make an item of clothing look smarter and more expensive than it really is.

And if, at the end of all that, you still prefer dry-cleaning, just make sure you find a good service and stick to it. I've had too many special items ruined from being caught on the hop in a place where I didn't have a recommendation for a decent dry-cleaner, or used the hotel service while I was on holiday or a work trip (thinking five stars meant a five-star clothes-cleaning service as well … wrong!).

Be considerate towards your delicate things when you're wearing them, and fix snags, holes and missing buttons or embellishment as soon as you can after they occur. Don't forget to hang up your clothes or lay them flat (and clean) when you take them off—it makes me sad to see the way some people fling their precious items on the floor. And use wooden or padded hangers: wire hangers are nasty, and will ruin the shoulders of your blouses, jackets and frocks over time. Show your clothes a little love, and I promise they'll repay you in loyalty.

When I grow bored of certain special items, I often store them away for a season or two, between sheets of acid-free tissue paper and topped with a sachet of dried lavender. That way, I almost forget I own them for a time, and can look at them with fresh eyes when I do decide to take them out again from their hiding place. If they're really useful pieces, I'll often have sought them out soon after storing them anyway, but it's nice to have some distance to appreciate your old clothes afresh.

When you've only a small amount of cash to spend on clothes, it's important to keep them in the best shape you possibly can with good washing, storage and TLC. That way, your clothes will last the distance and save you more in the long run.

Bygones be bygones alterations

Many hard-core vintage aficionados don't like the idea of chopping up clothes from another era, but I'm of the opinion that if it extends the life of the item and encourages you to wear it, why not? Far too many garments gather dust in our wardrobes because they're being saved for a special occasion, or because we're too afraid to alter them when they no longer fit, just in case we ruin them.

Altering the length of sleeves or chopping off seriously dowdy lengths of fabric to create an altogether more hip hemline, for example, is the easiest way to customise your clothes and bring them up-to-date in minutes. I'm always experimenting in this way, and often find myself falling totally in love with an item again, following a good snip or raised hem.

If you're feeling really lazy, you don't even need to hem the new lengths you've created; rough, raw edges are going through a real revival; you just need the *chutzpah* to carry it off. And if you ask me, an unfinished hem—especially on layers of floaty silk, chiffon or tulle (which doesn't need to be hemmed anyway)—has a certain boho charm. Raw edges can also look quite conceptual and arty when applied to the more structural of pieces, such as suit jackets, blazers and crisp cotton shirts, although I prefer a stitched hem myself.

Go on: be brave—especially if you're considering getting rid of something. There's no time like the present!

FAR TOO MANY GARMENTS GATHER DUST BECAUSE THEY'RE BEING SAVED FOR A SPECIAL OCCASION

Ingenious embellishment

I have the most gorgeous navy 3.1 Phillip Lim top; a basic silk tank adorned with a cluster of tiny gold beads that spell out *ciao*. I love it to bits, and it's such a simple idea (executed immaculately, of course). I often find inspiration in the form of lolly-like fripperies; things such as silk roses, sequinned starfish or a tattered black feather or two.

When you're on the prowl for fripperies, take a walk on the wild side and indulge your inner peacock. Bear in mind, though, that it's easy to go over-the-top … so many fashion disasters occur from a case of too much, rather than too little. But employed wisely, a touch of decoration can transform a plain little frock, top or pair of pants into pure fashion genius. And they can be a great way to cover up unwelcome stains, cigarette burns or moth holes as well.

Throw a dye-fest

When I was a hapless teenager, just out of home, it took me a while to master the whole separating-whites-from-darks-from-colours business when I did the weekly wash. I ended up with a pile of grubby looking items to wear for those first months.

That's when I discovered the beauty of hand-dyeing; I loved how colour could give new life to tired-looking clothes, or utterly transform something from its neutral shade. It also gave a particularly zingy lift to wool jumpers, silk Chinois-style tops and simple cotton or lace underwear. I've always thought a rosy pink bra strap under a white cotton shift or a lavender petticoat peeking out from under a hyacinth frock looks so pretty. And there's something lovely about the mottled effect that deliberately careless hand-dyeing gives to old, crushed silk.

You need to get yourself in the mood for a dye-fest, because it's messy and time-consuming—make sure you've got at least a couple of hours to burn, and very few distractions. It's also a little addictive, because you never know exactly how an item's going to turn out. That's the beauty of dyeing—sometimes the results are amazing, sometimes less so; but it's always fun to see the transformation. The thrill of successfully reinventing a previously boring or unattractive item always has me rifling through the closets, pulling more and more things out to experiment with. Go nuts, I say.

If you're adventurous, you could even attempt making the dye yourself from organic products such as vegetables, leaves and the like (for d[ye]vine inspiration, check out India Flint's wonderful book, *Eco Colour,* which shares lots of ideas on how to do just that).

The most commonly found dye—available in chemists, supermarkets and haberdashery stores—should take to anything made from 100 per cent natural fibres, so that means wool, linen, silk and cotton. Acrylic mixes can be a bit of an unknown quantity, but many will also take dye—to a degree. You can buy specially made dye for polyester and synthetics, but read the back of the packs carefully to make sure you're taking the right one home (I've bought the wrong dye on more than one occasion … read the fine print!).

Give your items a good wash first, to make sure there are no invisible marks or spills (especially if something is brand new), and you can pop them in the dye vat, still damp. Each brand of dye will come with its own instructions on how much water to add, ratios to use, etcetera. Most suggest adding a cup of salt to the mix to lock the colour in. Don't forget to wash your hand-dyed pieces separately from then on, just in case the colour runs; it shouldn't, but I'm always careful—best to pop it on a delicates setting from now on.

Lay your dyed pieces out in the shade to dry, after rinsing out the dye until the water runs clear. It's as simple as that.

Calling in the cavalry

In complete contrast to what I've just said—and the purpose of this book—there are some times when you simply must look to the professionals for help. There's no shame in admitting to your limitations, after all. I certainly did when I needed to transform the most important frock of my life, to date: my 1980s silk-taffeta wedding dress.

My husband and I got engaged in winter on a mountain top in Scotland, just outside Inverness. We were away for a lazy weekend with friends, and miles away from any decent shops. Being a hopeless frockaholic, I went nearly mad in the following few days before we arrived back in London. I was *desperate* to start shopping for The Dress.

After we returned, I took some time to wend my way up and down the King's Road, searching for a possible frock option. I finally wandered into the gloom of Steinberg and Tolkien, the famed vintage clothing boutique, only to be informed by a shop assistant that they were having a sale ... on wedding dresses.

The helpful woman led me downstairs to the basement, where racks and racks of secondhand frocks in every shade of ivory imaginable stretched out before me ... My brain went into meltdown before eventually settling on a massive, Princess Diana-style 1980s number with huge, ham-hock sleeves, a train, and shockingly abundant ruffles. But I couldn't help it. When I saw the crisply elegant, Chantilly cream-coloured fabric, it had me at *hello*.

Then I found myself a fabulous seamstress who was a specialist costumier for West End theatre productions. She whipped my dress into shape—starting with the bustier, which needed to be enlarged with a number of discreet panels (my frock's previous owner was *teensy*), and those sleeves, which were transformed into an Elizabethan-style, halter-neck ruff. My lovely seamstress also slimmed down the skirt, chopped off the train and gathered it at the back to give the dress a sleeker, willowy effect at the front. The woman was worth her weight in gold.

Next stop: the dry-cleaner. After languishing for twenty years or more in a wardrobe and dusty store, and after all those alterations, it needed a good clean and press, and some attention in the form of military uniform-grade starch to its accordion-pleated ruffles.

Voila, my dress was completed. And it went for another clean when the deed was done. On each occasion, I was happy as a clam entrusting it to the professionals.

One day I might have my wedding dress dyed and shortened, to create a dashing cocktail frock. I have a feeling it will look a little Lanvin in flavour if I do ... maybe the shade of indigo, emerald green, or plum. Or maybe I'll just keep it stored in its substantial box, between layers and layers of acid-free tissue paper, hidden at the top of our wardrobe for decades. Waiting, just waiting, for my daughter to decide whether she might wear it herself one day.

THERE'S NO SHAME IN ADMITTING TO YOUR LIMITATIONS

An Edwardian opera coat with typical lace appliqué
and dramatic frills and flounces, lined in silk–satin
and embellished with rhinestone buttons.

A heavily embroidered costume coat in kimono style,
circa 1910–1920. Purchased in Prague and believed
to have originally come from Russia, where the
Ballets Russes was formed.

CLASSIC
Belle Epoque and Edwardian Fashions

Prior to World War One, fashion was resolutely opulent, indulgent and concerned with parading one's wealth. Clothing was effectively employed as one of the most potent status symbols, with items heavily adorned with luxurious embellishments and made from the finest materials available, if you were blessed with the income to afford them. Garments of silk, satin, chiffon, voile, brocade, damask and lace all broadcast the wearer's social class before a word was spoken.

Even with the heaving bosoms (so beautifully depicted in Merchant Ivory period films), the fashionable 'S bend' silhouette was a conservative one, and created using restrictive corsets threaded with whale bone. Such highly impractical style was suited to a luxurious life, and for those fortunate enough not to have to work.

This period of romantic ideals was reflected in the colour choices for clothing, with white, pink and baby blue common. Women wore a number of elaborate outfits throughout the course of the day, dependent upon occasion. There were tea gowns, driving suits and evening gowns, to name but a few and, indeed, women spent large portions of their time dressing, with the aid of the domestic help to shape them into their restrictive clothing and corsets.

Director Sergei Diaghilev's 1910 season of the Ballets Russes became an overwhelming influence to artisans and designers until the late 1920s. Artists such as Picasso and Matisse were commissioned to produce the highly decorative performance costumes, which in turn influenced the fashions of the time with their embroidery details, kimono shapes and rich tapestries.

WORK THE LOOK

Clothing from this era is rare and can fetch many thousands for a single piece, but it's still possible to find something for a song in poor condition. For extremely delicate pieces with shattered silk and torn lace, you could contact the Lace Guild to help with professional restoration, or repair minor tears yourself with small, careful stitches mimicking any previous repair jobs. The same goes for embroidery— match thread at a haberdashery, or embroider over holes with era-appropriate designs.

Silk can be strengthened with iron-on bonding, and missing beads carefully matched and replaced. But I would caution against full reconstruction, which might destroy the antique charm of a piece. Wear your pieces with pride, paired with modern hair, make-up and accessories to avoid a Miss Havisham-style fashion faux pas.

The most commonly found and inexpensive items from the era are cotton and linen undergarments, because they were made to withstand rigorous washing: try soaking in nappy cleaning solution and hanging out—unrinsed—in the sun to dry. This should remove any yellowing or age stains. After the sun treatment, rinse well and dry in the shade.

For more ornate pieces, you could unpick sleeves or widen arm holes. These are particularly restrictive on antique items, as they were often tailored to fit extremely close to the body to show off a woman's arms and hands (with so much hidden, the small amount of skin on display formed an erotic focal point, and exposed wrists were the height of sexual allure).

If you're lucky enough to have inherited an antique dress or two from a great-grandmother or distant aunt, consider detaching the skirt and stitching on a length of grosgrain ribbon at the waistband, with enough length spare to tie in a bow at the back. This would look amazing for a special event, worn with a simple blouse or bodysuit. Or carefully remove its lace collar and reapply to a modern frock.

And if you're too nervous to do any of these, simply hang your antique item on a wooden hanger from the picture rail, so you can admire it daily for the work of art it is.

1960's orange satin party dress $7

Seriously
Fabulous
FROCKS

THE FROCKS HAD TO COME FIRST BECAUSE, IN MY BOOK, they're the ultimate fashion staple. It's the single most simple item to throw on and—with the addition of a few accessories—breeze out the door in, looking well put together, to boot. Whenever I'm hunting through flea markets or vintage boutiques, I always make a beeline for the dresses, assessing each one carefully for its potential before moving on to the separates and other accoutrements. A jumpsuit or playsuit offers the same speedy fashion fix (depending on how good your figure is), but I always feel like I'm wandering about in my jim-jams when I'm in a onesie.

It's not easy finding pre-loved frocks that fit perfectly, particularly when they're from the 1960s or earlier. There are a few reasons for this. For example, the female form has changed a lot over the past fifty years or so—we're larger in the bust, smaller in the hips and taller in general.

Mass-production of clothes was still relatively new back then, so most clothing was, effectively, couture, and much of it still handmade. The notion of standard dress sizes for segments of the population is a fairly new one. Can you imagine living in a time when you owned so few outfits that they all fitted neatly into one small, freestanding wardrobe? It wasn't that long ago … The built-in robes we have nowadays—indeed, the walk-in styles which take up an entire room (in my dreams)—would once have been the sole province of film stars and royalty.

And this is precisely why buying a vintage frock can be such a bargain: when people owned fewer clothes, they spent more on each item, investing in quality fabrics and workmanship with some promise of lasting the distance. They painstaking lined and laundered clothes, and crafted beautiful embellishments for decoration when times were too austere for jewels or luxurious swathes of fabric. It's simply not cost-effective to make clothes the same way these days, and with such attention to detail. And as so few of us have the time or inclination to make our own, we're likely to part with a small fortune in high-end boutiques for an item of clothing made to the same level of standards. Which I'm all for, once in a while—I just can't do it often enough to satisfy my almost-daily urge for a new look! However, when I buy a frock from a charity store or flea market, or invest in a relatively inexpensive item (compared to a brand new designer piece) from a vintage boutique, I can.

Now I'm going to let you in on a little secret. It's not a spectacularly clever idea— quite commonsense, really—but almost *every* frock, when made from the right foundations in the first place (and by that I mean lovely wool, cotton, silk, velvet or something else particularly delicious, in a nice shade or print), is worth reinventing. Too small? Add a panel. Too big? Perfect, more material for you to play with. Plain Jane? Add appliqué, beading, ribbons and myriad other fripperies to jazz her up. Too busy? Tone it down by removing things one at a time. Too long in the hem or the sleeves? Chop, chop. Damaged? Excellent, it'll cost even less to buy, and you can splash out on some divine embellishment to cover up the holes or stains or whatever contributed to its ruination. Or take off the outdated length and use the extra fabric to artfully patchwork your purchase. Or, if all else fails, part the top from the skirt to create separates.

Remember: nothing says glamour like a spectacular frock, and vintage *frou* is the very best kind.

Work in PROGRESS

My '20s-era frock was trashed! The first step was to cover raw sleeve edges with satin bias.

The straps of this '30s slip were attached with safety pins. I snipped off old straps and replaced with grosgrain ribbon.

Seriously damaged '30s frock, prior to total overhaul. Cover stains, shorten hemline and replace buttons.

A '70s dress with terrible stains, disguised with deep red dye and a patch of appliqué rose fabric.

Remnant silk with striking feather design — attach to '60s beaded top to create mini-dress.

I snipped the hem of this silk Wiggle to cover tears at back with iron-on bonding, and covered fraying hems with satin bias.

A total sack! I snipped off sleeves, added drastic tailoring and removed the ugly faux gem button.

✳ Each piece tells you what it needs: base decisions on what will work best for the fabric and fall of the garment.

The Showstopper

The showstopper doesn't need to be any particular style—just one which suits you and makes you feel a million bucks. It's *the* dress to make an entrance in, Grace Kelly or Audrey Hepburn-style, or when you want to channel the sass of Carrie Bradshaw strutting down Fifth Avenue. But don't expect to know it when you see it because, in its original state, your ultimate party frock probably needs a complete overhaul.

To find a showstopper, look to pre-loved frocks designed with momentous occasions in mind: old prom, formal or debutante dresses, 1980s ball gowns and cocktail numbers, bridesmaids' frocks and—of course—wedding dresses. They're usually made well, and with luxe fabrics such as raw silk, satin or velvet. And they often boast an abundance of material and embellishment for you to experiment and play with. Remember, it's not always what you add to an item—sometimes infinite improvements are made by what you take away.

My showstopper was a 1950s wedding dress I found in a flea market. Lined and pouffed with several layers of damaged tulle under the long, full skirt, it was decorated with a dusting of tiny glass beads and a row of covered buttons trailing down its spine. Many of the beads and buttons were falling off and rust-like age stains were spotted all over—effectively banishing it from being the future star of any white weddings. The sleeves were long, and loosely fitted.

CUSTOMISATION

With so many missing beads, I knew I would need to replace some before any other restoration took place. Matching the beads to new ones found at a haberdashery, I added them until I was happy with the result. Then came the dyeing.

My first thoughts were to transform my little number—let's call her Sascha—with a deep emerald green, or the blushing red of camellias, but those rust stains were rather bothersome ... you can't go past black for a timeless showstopper. The silk taffeta had a bit of a dusty look to it after dyeing, from the fibres being agitated throughout the process, but I decided that I actually quite liked the suede-like effect. If your showstopper is silk and you prefer a shinier look, you can try having your dress rebloomed at a professional dry-cleaners. This is where they add an oil-like solution to the fabric which brushes the fibres down flat again. It gives silk back its lustre, although not always quite the sheen it had before dyeing.

After the dye process, I shortened the skirt's hemline to expose the delicate layers of un-ironed tulle beneath, rolling over the raw edge and stitching along the hem. I slit the sleeves open along the inside seam of each arm and shortened them, before stitching them together again to make them more fitted—only by a couple of centimetres, but this made a surprising improvement to the overall look.

LOOK TO PRE-LOVED
FROCKS DESIGNED
WITH MOMENTOUS
OCCASIONS IN MIND

Party
like it's 1929

EVEN THOUGH THIS FROCK IS SOMBRE— A MODEST AFFAIR IN BLACK CREPE—THE DETAILS POSITIVELY SING ...

Oh, for a glimpse into the Jazz Age ... I would visit in a second to taste the music, the elegance and—above all—the fashion.

This is the only piece I still own from the 1920s, although I've loved a few others (to death, unfortunately) in my time. Even though this frock is sombre—a modest affair in black crepe— the details positively sing, and I always feel so *swellegant* when I'm wearing it. I've yet to find an appropriate cloche hat to complete the look, but there's no need: this dress is timeless as is, and needs little else in the way of adornment apart from a softly wound chignon ... even if it does make me wish I smoked, so I could sport one of those long, silver cigarette holders between perfectly manicured fingers.

RESTORATION

It would have been sacrilege to change the classic shape of this dress, but it did need lots of work before it was fit to go to parties again. The fabric was jaggedly torn in spots (most badly on the front bodice), the collar was stained blue in places (goodness knows how), the buttons and buckles tarnished, and missing many of their original diamantes, and the sleeve hems were both raw (likely from unpicked sleeves).

My first step was to source a replacement buckle and buttons for the drop-waist. The buckle I chose is new, with a vintage feel, and the buttons are vintage (unpicked from an old cardigan, gone many moons ago). I carefully removed the old ones from the delicate fabric, and added each new item in its place.

Next, I added a lightweight iron-on bonding behind the tears, to stabilise the fabric. I added four patches in total, backed with thin black silk to mask the gaps in the material. I then added a strip of bias-binding (which matches the antique lace collar) to the armholes, and ironed it down flat.

Last of all, I very carefully washed the collar by hand with a stain-removing soap and allowed it to dry before ironing flat.

A gown fit for a Goddess

Who doesn't secretly love a little underwear as outerwear? I'm not talking skimpy bras and dominatrix corsets in place of tops (hello, Madonna), or a wanton disrespect for pants in public (yes, I'm referring to you, Lady Gaga), but elegantly reinvented shapewear, and slips worn as frocks. The construction of undergarments plundered from less-permissive eras is far more demure than many of today's clothes, so why not? No-one will know, and if they do, kudos for channelling your inner minx.

Here are three absolutely stunning taffeta slips from the 1930s—I often wear them as evening dresses and doubt anyone's ever noticed they were designed for a different purpose. It was the era of the slinky, bias-cut goddess gown, after all. The first, as you can see from the 'before' photo, was badly ripped and in need of TLC. And despite her deliciously long, full skirt, she was such a Plain Jane. I've turned her into an attention-grabbing ball gown with some simple customisation.

Slip two is made from a coral moire taffeta, and was originally a bit grubby from age. I brightened up the colour with a good wash and stain remover, concentrating on its marks, and added a silk panel at the back where it plunged too far. I also added matching yo-yos with button details to its front. Paired with a slip underneath, it's definitely a successful case of underwear as outerwear.

Slip number three, a shimmering blue-gold, was virtually perfect as is, even though I think it was once worn under a matching lace dress, rather than on its own. I covered up a small, stubborn oil stain on one of the straps with a velveteen flower, and she was good to go. Don't you think she has such screen-siren glamour? She puts me in mind of Veronica Lake.

There's also nothing to stop you shortening the hemline of a too-long slip. I thought it a shame to lose any of the fabric from these lovelies, but may one day turn the black one into a knee-length cocktail frock, and add a fifties petticoat (or not … decisions, decisions).

Tip: It's always worth trying to shift oil stains—you never know how recent they were. If you spill oil on your outfit, apply a small dab of eucalyptus or tea tree oil before washing it in the machine or by hand. I go through a small bottle of eucalyptus oil each year, and use it at least once a week—it makes clothes smell truly gorgeous (and tea tree oil does the same trick).

THE CONSTRUCTION OF UNDERGARMENTS PLUNDERED FROM LESS-PERMISSIVE ERAS IS FAR MORE DEMURE THAN MANY OF TODAY'S CLOTHES

CUSTOMISATION

This full-skirted slip had a scary amount of tiny moth holes dotted all over when I found her in a flea market, so my first step was to pop her in a plastic bag in the freezer to kill any possible moth eggs hiding in the numerous folds.

A day later, and after a good wash, I snipped off the straps and replaced them with this vintage French grosgrain ribbon (given that one of the straps was hanging on with the aid of a safety pin, and the other by mere threads). I tried on the dress and carefully pinned the ribbons in place, taking care to position them to cover my bra straps (if you don't wear a bra, lucky you: ignore my advice and pop those babies wherever you like!). I know this sounds obvious, but it's a good idea to try the dress on with the bra you'll eventually wear it with, as strap placements differ between bras—you'd be amazed how many times I've attached new straps while wearing the wrong bra and had to readjust them, cursing not so quietly all the while. Sew straps in place by hand or on the machine.

I've also added a lovely crimson beaded and sequinned flower burst. I tried quite a few other options, but settled on this to go with the straps—plus, red and black can be quite a winning combination, don't you think?

Tip: If you're at all worried about moths (and you should be—the nasty beggars have a knack for destroying the very best knits and silks if left to their own devices), pop your item of clothing in a plastic bag and store in the freezer for twenty-four hours to kill any eggs laid in the fabric. I do this with every secondhand clothing item I bring into the house, just to be safe.

Paris Match Dress

When I was learning French, I used to buy copies of Gallic gossip magazine *Paris Match* for a little light relief. Written in relatively simple language, it was less dry than a textbook, easier to translate than a proper novel, less brain-frying than an existentialist tract by Albert Camus (er, somewhat) and, when all else failed, I had fun looking through the pictures. Celebrity bust-ups, society scandals and lust-worthy fashion … it's all bliss to peruse in the bath or when having a pedicure, preferably with a rose-flavoured Ladurée macaron in the hand (I never said I was deep).

I call this little number my *Paris Match* dress because: a) I bought her in a dingy hole-in-the-wall vintage boutique near our hotel in Le Marais, the last time my husband and I visited the city on a romantic mini-break, and b) she embodies my ideal of modest French beauty, well made as she is with gorgeous silk lining and luscious printed cotton (which puts me in mind of the bayou). She looks divine paired with Repetto ballet flats (Audrey's handmade shoe of choice), a fifties petticoat and a charming Lucite or chain-handled bag. With the prim bow and knee-length hemline, this is the frock to be photographed in, scandal or *non* (I think you'd do it justice, Ms Bruni-Sarkozy). I wore it myself for a television appearance, with a frothy petticoat—it felt just right for a big audience. As you can tell from the 'before' shot, *le sac* has had a loving transformation. My husband was in *le shock* when he saw me try it on in that French boutique—it really was awful in its original state but I could see the potential.

Customisation

My first step was to unpick the sleeves. After disposing of them, I rolled over the raw edges and stitched them by hand around the perimeter of each armhole.

Given it had a lining with a separate layer of finest, wispiest silk, I didn't want to ruin the dress by sewing the two layers together and ending up with pulls down the sides. Instead, I turned the dress inside out, tried it on, and pinned *under* the lining for a fitted silhouette (so just the outer layer; the part worn closest to my skin at this point). I then unzipped the dress, stepped out carefully, and machine-sewed along the lines of the pins, removing them as I went.

There was ample fabric in the hand-stitched hem, so I let it down by a good two inches and stitched it up again by hand. This was to accommodate a fifties petticoat, but my *Paris Match* frock looks *jolie* worn with or without it.

Tip: *Consider how proper fitting will transform an item. This dress must have been overlooked countless times for its unflattering shape, but the fabric and details are exquisite. It cost about twenty euros—when it's hardly possible to make a frock from scratch for that, why let the lovely fabric go to waste?*

The new Wiggle

AUTHENTIC EARLY SIXTIES FROCKS SUCH AS THIS ARE FEW AND FAR BETWEEN—MOST LIKELY BECAUSE THEY WERE LITERALLY WORN TO DEATH

Mid-century frocks are fairly ubiquitous in vintage stores and antiques markets all over the place. But their cachet following the success of *Mad Men* and the recent Louis Vuitton-championed fifties revival means it's becoming that much harder to find top-condition pieces made from really appealing fabrics. A simple way to modernise a late fifties or early sixties frock is by shortening the hemline to create a mini, or at least a shorter version of the classic Wiggle dress (named for the wiggle in your walk when you wear one, and seen on minxy office manager Joan in *Mad Men*).

This silk Wiggle dress with a distinctive reddish-orange cabbage roses print was a real find. Authentic early sixties frocks such as this are few and far between—most likely because they were literally worn to death in the era.

You can see from the 'work in progress' images that this dress was badly stained around the underarms and showing significant signs of wear and tear, with coming-apart seams and frayed hems. The tissue-thin silk was also jaggedly torn in a few places at the lower back, just beneath the bottom.

Tip: *To tailor any dress you've found in a larger size, simply try it on inside out and insert bobble-headed pins evenly down the sides to shape it to your figure. Be careful not to prick yourself as you pull it back over your head—you may require some help from a friend. Those with a zipper down the back will be easier to shimmy out of.*

I love everything about this dress, from the fit to the fabric to the pintucks and considerate detailing—it even has those clever press-studs hidden under the shoulder straps to keep your bra in place. Given the choice, I wouldn't do a thing to change it, but it needed a host of repairs and a little freshening up to make it worthy of the book launch I wanted to wear it to. The bias edging was just the ticket to tidy up its unkempt edges and distract the eye from more prominent signs of use, without losing any of its authentic vintage charm.

CUSTOMISATION AND RESTORATION

Firstly, I gave the very delicate fabric a handwash in nappy cleaning solution, laying it in the dissolved solution in the bath without wringing, and hung it out in the sun to dry, without rinsing. This faded the considerable age and perspiration stains. I then rinsed it carefully, and waited for it to dry before repairing the large horizontal rip at the back. I did this by sewing a straight seam across one panel with my sewing machine, and reinstated the missing seam above the fishtail pleat with another row of stitching. The spot where the tear was thankfully allows the seam to be hidden (people shouldn't be staring closely enough at your derrière to notice it—then again, they probably are, because in this dress it will look *fabulous*). I then covered up the two smaller tears with swatches of fabric stolen from the original hem, as closely pattern-matched as possible, and with iron-on bonding and a few tiny stitches.

Next, I sourced thin, olive green bias-binding to cover the knackered seams around the neck, armholes and hemline. The colour picks out the shade of leaves in this handsome print. Lastly, I ironed the bias edging flat.

Tip: *Bias-binding can make a great feature on any item of clothing, and also strengthens and covers any weak or damaged hemlines and edges. Sew the bias to the outside of the garment with your machine, along one fold, before doubling over and stitching the other side by hand with small, firm stitches threaded through the inside of the bias ribbon for a super-professional finish.*

A pretty, much-restored watercolour-hued
Wiggle dress from Peck & Peck, New York.
I've taken up the sleeves and hemline, and
repaired the shattered silk at shoulders and
sleeves with appliqué taken from the redun-
dant hem fabric—a very similar repair job
to the cabbage roses frock. Silk patches were
applied with iron-on bonding, and sewn by
hand for added strength, and bias binding
added to frayed edges.

Alice (lives it up) in Wonderland

ALL I NEEDED TO ADD WAS FIFTIES-STYLE VOLUME TO AMP UP THE SILHOUETTE, AND THE GLAMOUR

Here's a simple idea for pulling off a properly fifties look: take a full-skirted frock or circle skirt and sew in a few layers of stiff tulle (for a petticoat), or buy a separate petticoat to wear with any full skirt.

I picked up this stunning frock from a flea market for small change. Made from beautiful pink and bronze Chinese brocade, it's possibly the best bargain I've ever found. I've worn it out countless times for high tea and dinner (most memorably, to cocktails and dinner at the Sydney Opera House—that was a *great* night).

Apart from a small stain, my frock was in near-perfect condition and fit like a dream, but with stiff interfacing under the skirt for structure it fell in an awkward shape without any petticoats beneath to puff it up. All I needed to add was fifties-style volume to amp up the silhouette, and the glamour. Plus a pretty brooch to cover the small stain on the bodice.

Pair with beaded gloves and a Betty Draper demeanour.

More tea, Vicar?
Tea Dress

A FORGIVING ITEM OF CLOTHING, BECAUSE ALTHOUGH THEY HAVE A NEAT, NIPPED-IN WAIST, THE SPRIGGY FLORALS TEND TO DRAW ATTENTION AWAY FROM FIGURE FLAWS

Around about the time *The Edge of Love* was released (a gloriously moody film about the poet Dylan Thomas, his wife, and his lover, played by Sienna Miller and Keira Knightley respectively), 1940s tea dresses made a comeback—preferably paired with Hunter wellies and a chunky, hand-knitted cardigan the shade of heather or mustard. That's when I went in search of a vintage rather than mass-market chainstore version (although Topshop brought out some excellent little frocks I did consider buying).

Tea dresses are a forgiving item of clothing, because although they have a neat, nipped-in waist, the spriggy florals tend to draw attention away from figure flaws (particularly of the lower-half variety; pears, a tea dress is your friend) and mask any marks. They're also easy to darn without ruining (those flowery prints hide a thousand sins) and rarely need an iron. In hardy cotton, they make a great everyday house frock and, indeed, I have several for just that purpose which can be thrown on in haste and wash and dry without fuss.

For everyday ease, pair with the aforementioned no-nonsense boots and cardi, or simple sandals,

belt at the waist and wear with a Panama hat—this is a great summer music festival outfit (slip a pair of tights in your clutch to pop on when the temperature drops). For a more glamorous take, switch the wellies and chunky knit for a velvet bolero and T-bar heels.

Although I'd call it a tea dress, this little number didn't originally start life that way because she's not from the forties. I found her in an overcrowded retro clothing store looking tired and unloved, and imagined the previous owner as a 1980s secretary, complete with flick haircut, tan stockings and pair of hexagonal-framed glasses. I may have whistled Dolly Parton's theme tune for '9 to 5' as I withdrew her from the rack.

My frock had the classic forties features which experienced a burst of popularity in the eighties, but in an exaggerated form, with excessively large shoulder pads, overly puffy shoulders and a mid-calf hemline. The skirt was entirely shapeless, and fell unflatteringly, and I spied a few small tears when I held it up to the light.

CUSTOMISATION

The first action I took was to snip out the shoulder pads, but this left me with too-wide shoulders. However, I liked the gathering at the sleeve head, and didn't want to lose this effect—the dress still fit fine under the armpits. Rather than unpicking the sleeves and re-attaching them, I tried the dress on first, and studied it in the mirror. I pinched together the fabric at the top edge of my left shoulder blade by a few inches and folded the excess underneath, which gave it a gathered but more rounded and well-fitting sleeve, and an altogether less blousy appearance. I pinned the fabric in place, making sure the excess was tucked inside the fold. I repeated the action with the right shoulder.

Turning the dress inside-out, I machine-stitched the fabric together as closely as possible to the gathering at the edge of each sleeve (in a straight line), and followed the shape of the sleeve around until it met the original stitching underneath the armpit, leaving a loop of fabric at the edge. Applying another line of stitching, but this time in a zig-zag stitch, I then snipped off the excess fabric to create crescent-moon-shaped remnants.

I tried on the dress again and checked out the hemline with the new shoulders—still too long and shapeless. Folding the hem underneath, I raised and pinned it until I was happy with the result, deciding on a spot part-way up the thighs. Chopping off the excess fabric and rolling the raw edge under, I stitched the new hemline into place. I tried it on again inside-out, then pinned the sides of the waist in on either side, as well as up the sides towards the bust and partly down the skirt. Removing pins as I sewed, I stitched up the seams for a fitted waistline, leaving the excess fabric inside the dress (just in case I wanted to unpick it at a later date).

Locating the tears, I hand-stitched them with dark thread. Carefully pulling together the edges, I used small stitches to pull the fabric together and, when done, ironed it as flat as possible to mask the pulls in the frock's natural fall. And there you have it: one completed tea dress!

Tip: To mask any repair darning, use thread in a darker shade than your fabric. Thread the same colour or lighter will be more visible. For larger tears, use backing fabric and iron-on bonding to stabilise the fabric.

Here's my genuine forties tea dress, which I've done very little to apart from repairing tears to the delicate silk under the arms, and taking up the hem. While my 1980s version is hardier, this one I save for more refined events than mooching about the house, such as high tea with the girls or a picnic in the park.

The Secretary
runs the show

I adore a sexy secretary look … think Maggie Gyllenhaal in the kooky romance, *The Secretary*. Saucy temptress, with hidden depths and vulnerability.

Hunt for forties or eighties dresses when you're looking for the foundation of modern secretary style, or elegant office wear; those ladies did it best. Easy to find are the eighties blousy numbers, overegged with pussy-bows and calf-length hemlines. They're perfect for chopping up and restyling, what with all that extra fabric going on, but steer clear of the cheap synthetics so mass-produced throughout the era and opt for silk georgette, cotton or wool (or at least silk, cotton or wool-mixes if you can find them—much less likely to make you perspire in a sticky situation).

If you're lucky enough to find pieces in your size and in good condition, the 1940s secretary style offers a more chic and streamlined look. Compact, rounded shoulder pads, fitted bustlines and beguiling pintucks and detailing mean there's little to change but the damage sustained by decades of wear.

Sexy Secretary is a woollen forties frock, which was in fairly good condition apart from a few bad stains down the skirt and tiny moth holes dotted all over. I adore the scalloped piping, a very rare detail. It must have taken an age to sew into the skirt, and tailor so finely at the shoulders. Who wouldn't get the position, wearing this to a job interview?

Originally a grubby mid-coral colour, I've dyed this frock to a lovely shade of purplish-mauve to mask the skirt stains, and repaired holes by hand. I removed the clear glass beads which cover each press-stud at the top of the spine first, and reattached them after dyeing to prevent staining, and strengthened all the press-studs at the side and back with hand-stitching.

I call her Ingrid (as in Bergman, of course).

Psychedelic Revival

WEAR SIXTIES FROCKS TO PARTIES AND AROUND THE HOUSE WHEN THE DAY CALLS FOR A LITTLE COLOUR INJECTION

I'm quite partial to a bit of sixties psychedelia. I had various polyester numbers in a riot of clashing shades when I was younger; from a twisted print of baby pink, lime and lemon which hurt the eyes to take in, to a tangerine, lilac and chartreuse frock which put me in mind of that spinny-headed, sick feeling you get after one too many trips on a theme park rollercoaster. I wore them everywhere on my beanpole adolescent frame, and loved to boogie the night away at favourite club nights, The Tender Trap and Sounds of Seduction, with fire-engine red hair.

I even went through a phase of wearing longer versions of the classic 1960s cocktail frock more recently. That is, until I caught sight of my reflection in an airport lounge mirror, and had a moment's realisation that, bar the missing beehive, I looked like an extra from a *Carry On* film—oh, dear.

These days, I'm into toned-down versions which still reference the era and psychedelic vibe, but aren't too eye-popping. And I've ditched the polyester for good or lined it with breathable cotton, wearing my sixties frocks to parties and around the house alike when the day calls for a little colour injection.

CUSTOMISATION

This fluorescent pink silk mini dress has a simple black and blue print which isn't too overwhelming. It used to be too wide in the arms and waist, but I've slimmed it down a little with an extra seam down the inside arm and sides to create a more fitted look, and also shortened the hemline.

You can see I've added a bit of glam, fifties flavour with this sequin and bead collar, stitched on by hand with needle and thread. I bought the collar in a lighter tone of purplish-pink, pre-made from a haberdashery. It wasn't the right shape for the frock's neckline, but I quite liked the feature of bringing it down by an inch or two—it almost looks like a matching sequinned necklace.

Tip: To avoid the feel of nasty acrylic on your skin, line polyester or nylon pieces with a very light cotton, or wear with a fitted slip—this also helps mask bumps on less-than-perfect figures.

Flower child
Mini Dress

There's something so fresh and fun about wearing an A-line frock and sandals in high summer when you're fifteen, walking along listening to 'Itchycoo Park' or 'California Dreamin'' on a bright yellow Sony Walkman—that was me. I still own countless versions in tissue-thin Swiss cotton with huge daisy prints all over, working the free love vibe when it's too hot to do much else.

This is one of my favourite summer frocks. I wear her on days when the temperature soars, with strappy metallic leather sandals for hunting through flea markets, and to the beach because it's light, airy, and washes so easily. She dresses up easily in the evening with a pair of heels, beaded cashmere cardigan and some costume sparklers, or moves easily into trans-seasonal wear with opaque tights, go-go boots and a long, drapey cardi. A versatile little number, that's for sure.

CUSTOMISATION

I'm convinced this dress was originally a maternity piece, because it had such large panels at the front and was nowhere near as short as the permissive era allowed. I took in the panels quite a lot at the front, disposing of the unnecessary extra fabric, and took up the hemline by about four inches so it now sits mid-thigh. If I were fifteen again, it would be bottom-grazing, but such pin-strutting wouldn't be seemly at my age.

Come back, Edie!  Shift

I've lost count of the amount of beaded tanks I've lovingly worn, and worn out, over the years. I remember a time, back in the nineties, when they were considered so gauche you could find them on every charity store rack. Clearly, the cool of Edie Sedgwick had been forgotten. Now, they're like the proverbial hen's teeth, fetching phenomenal prices when in excellent condition. These days, I own a grand total of six of the little beauties.

Despite the fact these beaded tops were created in the sixties, they often put me in mind of the roaring twenties. There's something distinctly flapper-ish about the beaded tassels and straight-up-and-down silhouette of a beaded tank. So versatile, it looks chic paired with a pencil skirt or palazzo pants, and similarly fab winking out from beneath a fitted jacket or bolero; even layered over a simple black dress. A beaded tank is also ready to party with the best of them when paired with a mini and heels, or happy to roam along city streets by day with high-waisted shorts, bare legs, ballet flats and a huge pair of dark sunnies.

With several of these glitzy little numbers hanging in my wardrobe, I decided to eliminate decision-making by turning one of two white versions I own into a dress. It's an embarrassingly simple idea, but effective for transforming a

THERE'S SOMETHING FLAPPER-ISH ABOUT THE BEADED TASSELS AND SILHOUETTE

glam sequinned top into a short, chic shift. It also works with those ubiquitous sequinned butterfly tops from the eighties (fast becoming a collector's item), if you're more a fan of those. I would totally wear this to a daytime pool party ... I just have to wait for an invitation to one which mirrors the excess of the twenties (LA's Chateau Marmont, anyone?). In the meantime, it's my go-to summer cocktail frock.

This type of beaded top is easy to turn into a shift dress, because it's rarely fitted around the waist, which allows the silk to fall in an unbroken line from its lower hem. The boxier, the better: look for a looser fit when on the hunt, if you don't own one already, and make up for the modest shape with a thigh-revealing hemline—I have. And don't think of it as a permanent decision: you can always unpick the silky lower half at a later date if you grow tired of it. Make a fetching hair tie to match. *Go-go,* Edie!

CUSTOMISATION

All you need in addition to the top is enough silk to create the skirt. I've used a lovely length picked up at a sample sale. I tried on the tank and used pins to attach the silk the entire way around, selvedge meeting the other raw edge of fabric at the back. I also used pins to mark the intended hem. Unzipping the tank, I stepped out carefully before pinning the back seam of the skirt in a straight line, wrong sides together.

Next, I machine-sewed the silk to the tank in one straight line. Then I sewed together the back seam, wrong sides together. I snipped off the excess fabric very close to the seam, before turning inside out to sew another line of stitching to create a French seam.

Lastly, I double-checked, then cut, the hem, rolling under the raw edge and stitching in a straight line the entire way around. If you want to give yourself a little extra, just in case you'd like to take the hem down at a later date, fold over more fabric, iron flat and stitch by hand with needle and thread.

To finish, iron the seams flat before admiring your crafty new shift dress in the mirror.

Two favourite tanks: a gold version I've added extra beaded stars to at the shoulders, where it was missing sequins and beading, and a rare indigo, white and gold patchwork-effect sequinned number.

Kaftan *Couture*

Being the mother of a small child, I feel right at home in kaftans, but I've been a devotee of the look since my mid-teens, when the look championed by Barbara Hulanicki's iconic London store, Biba, hit its first revival. Kaftans are loose-flowing and easy to move about in, forgiving on the figure, and lend a certain air of worldly sophistication with their ethnic overtones. Available in a huge range of styles, they're the perfect attire for moseying about the house, attending a pool party or (in the more ornate styles) stepping out in for cocktails and dancing.

Fashion designers around the globe started making kaftan-style dresses in the seventies—around the same time affordable air travel was introduced, sparking a culture of backpackers eager to explore previously far-flung destinations. Kaftans from the era abound in the vintage stores of hip neighbourhoods and inner-city flea markets. But I've usually found the best bargains—apart from those picked up on travels in India, Asia, Africa or the Middle East—can be found in the charity stores of country towns, the outer suburbs, and wealthy neighbourhoods; more conservative areas, where there's less demand for this hippie staple. And I never pass on the opportunity to visit traditional clothing stores in the areas where ethnic subcultures flourish. I'm fond of rummaging in Indian clothing and jewellery stores in particular, because I love the intricate decoration you'd pay a fortune for from a designer.

These kaftans are short to long-ish styles which look modern. I wear full-length kaftans around

LEND A CERTAIN AIR OF WORLDLY SOPHISTICATION WITH ETHNIC OVERTONES

the house because they have such laid-back charm, but I generally don't step out wearing one unless I want to work the full seventies vibe.

THE KAFTAN GOES MINI

I found this charcoaly-blue raw silk kaftan in a flea market, and have lost count of the number of times I've worn it out to dinner parties and dancing with friends. It inspired an impromptu night of dancing 'til dawn … following a 'quiet' mid-week night of tapas and sangria. The kaftan always puts me in mind of that lovely French icon, the original boho chick, Brigitte Bardot.

Originally so long in the hem that it swept the ground, my kaftan was covered in the type of holes and damage that indicate poor care—it must have been flung carelessly into a washing machine and chewed to pieces by the rough cycle. Raw silk *can* be tricky to look after; jewellery alone destroys the fabric when it catches. The previous owner must have been tiny in the bust and hips as well, so I turned the kaftan inside out and found there was ample leftover fabric in the seams for me to let it out—otherwise I would have walked away.

CUSTOMISATION AND RESTORATION

My first job was to chop off the sweeping hem and create a new one by rolling over the edges of the fabric and stitching it in a straight line. I was sad to do it, but the fabric was too holey and discoloured towards the bottom to do much else. I cut it as long as I could to preserve the top half (which, you can see, is still quite short). Then I painstakingly repaired, by hand, the few holes left in the top, and reattached the long zipper in the back with machine-sewing, as it had been coming away in places.

Next I let out the side seams. I did it *very* carefully, unpicking the stitches one at a time with a seam ripper and pulling the fabric apart ever so gently, trying not to create any extra holes. Trying it on inside-out, I popped pins along the open sides in a downwards direction. With help from my husband to undo the zipper and pull the kaftan up over my head, I machine-sewed along the sides following the line of pins, removing each one as I went.

I'd been wearing this frock for years before I visited a small store that stocked glass beads for jewellery-making. I bought a handful to create a necklace, and found a use for the leftovers in the front panel of stitching here.

Although she needs life-extending surgery once in a while, my reinvented kaftan is one of the most treasured items in my wardrobe, and I'll miss her to bits when she finally falls apart (but you can be sure I'll find a use for that embroidered front panel, somewhere …)

BOLLYWOOD, HERE I COME

Unlike the previous kaftan, which I suspect is a designer version (the label was missing when I bought it so it's too hard to tell, but the shape was flattering in the extreme and boasted a number of telltale features, such as immaculate stitching, figure-hugging darts and a hidden zip), this jungle green kaftan is definitely an Indian original. I know, because I bought it with the matching harem-style pants. Its style was too loose and shapeless to be anything but a traditional outfit—built for modest celebration, rather than wild seventies key parties.

CUSTOMISATION

As with the previous kaftan, I've injected this dress with a little sixties flavour. Chopped to a mini like the first, I also snipped off the wide, puffy sleeves to give it an A-line feel, rolling the fabric under and hand-stitching around the armholes to prevent fraying. I stitched the bottom hem on the machine using a special silk needle for the sheer chiffon.

Next up, I took the sides in by a good few inches, after first trying it on inside out and pinning evenly along the sides (you could also follow these steps on a dressmaker's model). To tailor the shape, I've created two darts in the lower back, one on each side of the spine. It now has a waist, without being too tight.

I adore the sequins and gold stitching on real Indian pieces, but often find they tip over the line into being too garish. The work on this piece was perfect—except for the cheap-looking plastic beads sewn in the middle of the chest. I replaced them with new beads and a flower sequin in tarnished gold, which improved its appearance in a small, yet important, way. Sometimes the tiniest alterations make the world of difference.

Karma Chameleon

ONCE BOASTING MASSIVE SHOULDER PADS AND A TRIANGULAR, SACK-LIKE SHAPE THAT TAPERED TO A MID-CALF HEMLINE, SHE WAS REMINISCENT OF A COSTUME IN A NEW ROMANTICS MUSIC VIDEO

This is another much-loved item in my wardrobe—she's seen me through untold escapades in restaurants and bars over the years. When I found her she was so badly dated, I could barely wait to get home and start customising. A flea market find, my frock boasted seriously massive shoulder pads and a triangular, sack-like shape that tapered to a mid-calf hemline, reminiscent of a costume in a New Romantics video clip. But the fabric was an exquisite matt silk I simply couldn't pass on—it must have been made for kimonos. I also found the Japanese design fetching, despite the fact it was a terrible fit. I can't imagine the style ever coming around again, but who knows? I'm certainly no fortune-teller when it comes to these things.

My favourite way to wear this frock is with a black bobbed wig, *à la* Uma Thurman in Tarantino's cult film *Pulp Fiction*, with a simple gold cuff at the wrist. It feels very eighties New York to me.

My favourite night out in this was when I wore it to world-class Japanese restaurant Tetsuya's, to celebrate my husband's birthday. I felt super-glamorous sporting it with a pair of towering heels and a coolly detached visage (well, I tried); think a character in a Bret Easton Ellis novel, played by a young Angelica Huston. We planned to go dancing, but a thirteen-course degustation, paired with wine, put a stop to our plans … James fell asleep on the short taxi journey to the club; I can just about remember the first part of the evening!

CUSTOMISATION

First I removed the shoulder pads with my trusty Quick Unpick. Then I tried the dress on inside out and pinned down the sides by a few inches, the whole way down each side seam. I didn't try to create a waist with this frock—I think I would have ruined the effect of the batwing sleeves if I had. Lastly, I chopped off the lengthy hem to mid-thigh. This effectively balanced out the width of the dress at the top for a more modern shape.

The lady loves
Flamenco

This seventies dress has *the* most fabulous shape. Cut like a dream, she falls beautifully and fans out sideways in a very satisfying manner when given a little twirl. Paola gives great skirt in any heated dance routine, so makes the perfect dress for flamenco-ing. Despite her fiery nature, she's cool as a cucumber. Take her to the club and watch the boys stare … *Olé!*

CUSTOMISATION

Originally ivory, I dyed this dress deep scarlet to cover a stubborn orange stain on the breast, and red-paint drips down the back; it also gave a lift to its overall grubby demeanour. The dye only darkened the mark at the front, but covered up the paint stains at the back. My solution—before dyeing it black to cover the stains altogether—was to see what an appliquéd corsage would look like.

I took a blush-coloured rose from an old 1950s tablecloth, chopping it out carefully to save the rest of the fabric for later. I pinned it over the stain with two bobble-headed pins before sewing around the perimeter with small, firm embroidery stitches. One rose seemed enough, but I was prepared to keep adding them and, indeed, the full bouquet could work well on another stained dress.

Lastly, I added a bronze Art Deco button I found in a French flea market. Paola wears it proud.

'PAOLA' FALLS
BEAUTIFULLY
AND FANS
OUT SIDEWAYS
IN A VERY
SATISFYING
MANNER
WHEN GIVEN A
LITTLE TWIRL

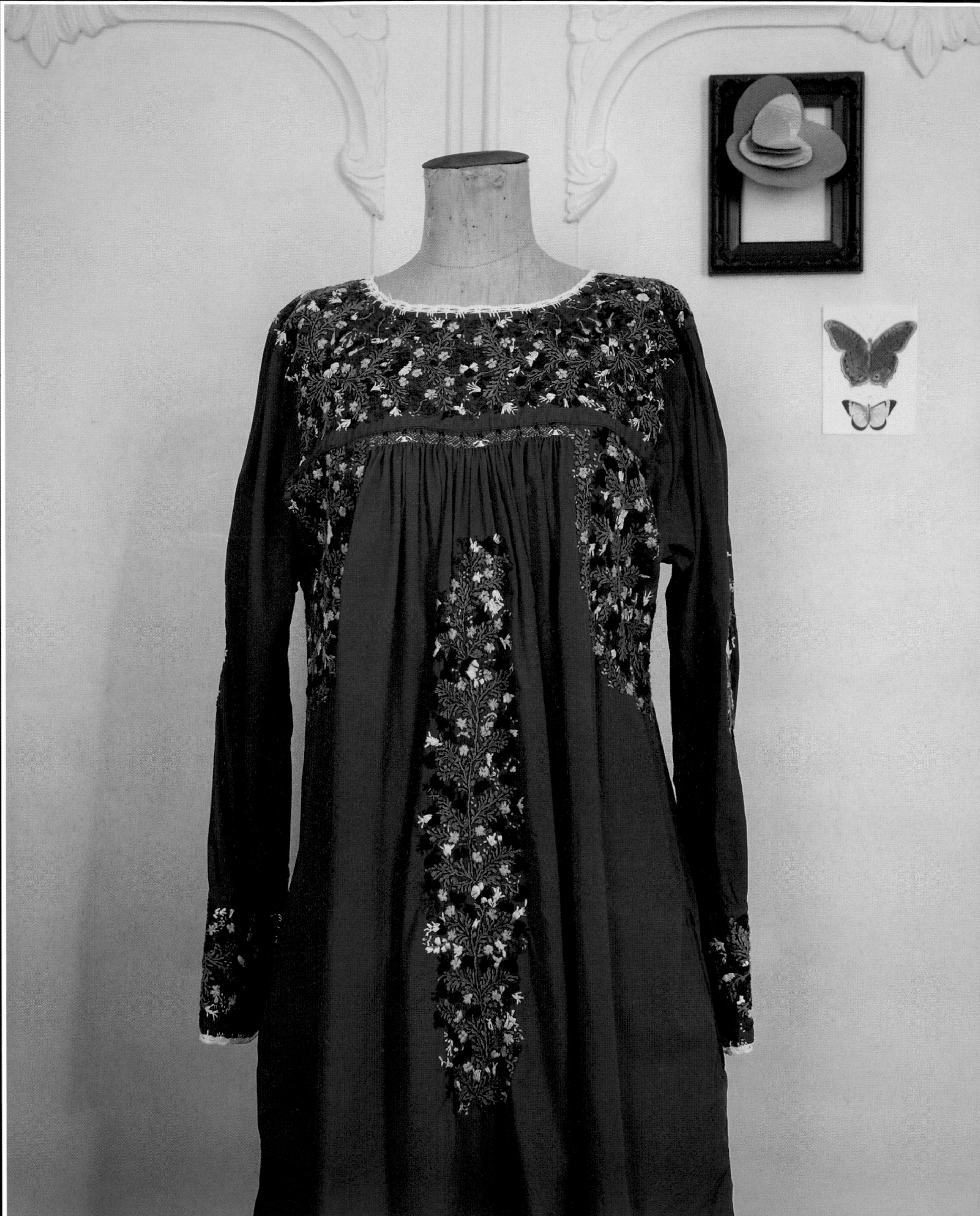

South of the border Smock

Mexican peasant dresses are another seventies staple—throw one on and you're ready in minutes. They ooze cute hippie charm and look fabulous worn with perfectly bronzed pins. If you're none too keen on baring your legs, peasant smocks are wonderful layered over jeans, leggings or opaque tights as a long top. A failsafe 'off duty' look with sandals and easy hair, these embroidered flowers are all the accessories you need.

My South of the Border smock's a winner for summer music festivals. The one major change I've made is to add pockets—I wanted to wear it to the aforementioned all-day festival of live bands without a tote to worry about. Pockets allowed me to shimmy freely, with just enough space for keys, cash, phone and lipgloss hidden in the folds of my dress.

I call her Stevie—she's so seventies, dahling.

CUSTOMISATION

When I bought this smock it had a raw hem—presumably it was once much longer. I rolled the raw edge over and stitched a straight hem the entire way around. The embroidery panels were bare in places, where threads had come loose and gone missing. I carefully matched the threads at a haberdashery, filling in the spaces with stitching and following the design from the rest of the smock. At the sleeves were green buttons, which I replaced with red ones (I'm not fond of red and green together … too Christmas-y).

For the pockets, I matched the fabric to some similar red cotton at a haberdashery. I cut the pockets out freehand, making sure they were deep enough to fit my hand, and with enough left around the outside for the seams. I sewed the sides of each pocket with a straight stitch before repeating with a zig-zag for strength; I didn't want to lose my keys in a field! I unpicked the sides of the smock to insert the pockets, sewing the smock and pocket together from the inside, and reversing a few times at the top and bottom to strengthen the seams.

Tip: If you need help creating pockets, just turn an item with pockets inside out, and follow their shape as a pattern.

Woodstock, here I come! Look closely at that embroidery: see those little people stitched into the breast panel? I think they're for luck, good crops or fertility … watch out!

Follow the
Sun Dress

There's something so appealing about an item of clothing which has survived through numerous generations, being altered along the way to suit each new recipient; new chapters added to its story. We rarely repair things these days, so it's a real joy to see the patience, love and history poured into such special pieces.

This cotton/viscose-mix sundress, with its classic 1930s floral print, is a perfect example of timeless tailoring. You can see, from the few 'before' snaps, how my frock had fallen on hard times. She—let's call her Edith—was ripped, badly stained, littered with moth holes, and fitted to suit at least two different women in her time (I know, because I unpicked layers of alterations around the waist and skirt to 'find' the original dress). The sleeves and neckline had been re-stitched goodness knows how many times, and any buttons she'd once had were long gone.

I doubt Edith had seen the light of day in decades, but by the time I wore her to high tea with a group of girlfriends, she looked good as new—better, in fact—and I was asked more than once where I'd found her.

What drew me to this frock was the humble patchworking at the right side of the bodice, which led me to believe she'd limped along as a house dress ... maybe only used to do the cleaning in (or with). I quickly saw how cleverly another piece of the same fabric (maybe from the sleeves?) had been used to patch over a stain at the breast. I took inspiration from the patchworked area and continued the theme all over, with pieces of fabric removed from the hem. I'm thrilled with the results. Can't you see her surviving for another eighty years or more?

RESTORATION

To create your own areas of interest with patchwork, see if there's any part of your frock you can remove, such as I've done here with the excess fabric from a long hem. Or you could go for patchworking which deliberately clashes with the original fabric—this works just fine; note, though, that this works better for prints than block colours ... all that print is quite forgiving, and makes patchwork look chic rather than cheap.

Cut out irregular shapes from the excess fabric and pin in place, securing with stitches around the edges. Here, I've copied the previous patchworker's style, using a machine zig-zag stitch around the edges and a line of straight stitching about a centimetre in, because I loved the look and saw no point in changing it.

For a tired, faded fabric such as this one, try a pretty silk flower in a zingy colour attached to the bodice or shoulder strap. It really lifts the finished look. This is now my ultimate summer sundress, to wear to a picnic with red ballet flats or my favourite Vivienne Westwood for Melissa shoes: a pair of towering, pale-blue heels topped with shiny red love hearts.

A satin drop-waist dress from the 1920s, festooned with
ornate French lace tiers and a ribbon sash common to
the era. Made before zippers were used on clothing, this
extravagant frock fastens with side snaps.

A plainer 1920s daywear option in salmon pink cotton with
dropped waist, scalloped collar and attached faux jacket.

CLASSIC  *Twenties*

After World War One, a new modernism enveloped fashion, with corsets and curves discarded in favour of a streamlined, androgynous and sporty ideal. Women bound their breasts and cut their hair short. Hemlines were raised and waists were dropped, backs were bared and arms and legs were shown, and transparent fabrics with ornate beading and lacework were used, giving rise to the risqué 'flapper'. It was a time of exuberance and showing off one's wealth, but also a time of thumbing one's nose at the dated ideals of previous generations.

Travel and exotic prints influenced fashion, with Egyptian and Art Deco references, and clothing was often accessorised with furs, long strands of beads and pearls. Designers such as Gabrielle 'Coco' Chanel epitomised the leap into this new era of fashion, with her fondness for expensive simplicity.

The boyish slant to the new feminine shape was no doubt influenced by the climate of war and the emancipation of women. Most women were required to fulfil at least a few traditionally masculine duties, having experienced whole generations of their menfolk away fighting on the battlefields. Victorian conservatism seemed outmoded to a generation jaded by the effects of war, and notions such as chaperones for females seemed ridiculous in light of women being forced to nurse the naked, battle-scarred bodies of so many returned soldiers.

WORK THE LOOK

The twenties look is a great one to embrace if you're in the early stages of pregnancy and still trying to hide it: drop-waists are very forgiving, and allow a baby bump to be concealed well into the third or fourth month, at least. It's also a good style for beanpole types with no curves, or those with thicker waistlines, particularly if you have a small bust.

If you are blessed with a tiny waist and ample curves, there's nothing to stop you wearing the dresses of the twenties, but why not add a thin belt at the waist to cinch things in? It's not true to the style of the era, but looks fabulous nonetheless. You could even add a permanent belt by sewing a length of ribbon into place at each side hem (do this by hand or with a longer stitch on your machine, so it can be unpicked easily at a later date if need be), and don't be afraid to raise hemlines and carefully detach unflattering, boxy sleeves (but save them, just in case you want to reattach later). Many hemlines came to below the knee, but raise yours if you prefer a snappy, tennis-on-the-lawn style.

For such time-worn pieces, nappy cleaning solution, iron-on bonding and needle and thread should form the basis of your restoration arsenal. Additionally, new bias-binding, buckles, buttons and beads, and a sewing machine with hardy cotton/polyester-mix thread (for going over all those ancient seams) will be invaluable. For overly plain pieces, adorn with beading or delicate embroidery for added flourish. And don't be scared to remove a little frou to make ornate pieces more wearable.

Nice day for a WHITE WEDDING

WHEN CHOOSING A DRESS FOR MY WEDDING DAY, VINTAGE wasn't my first choice. To be honest, I was a teensy bit superstitious about buying a discarded wedding frock, and dismissed the idea almost immediately. In the end, of course, I did opt for a secondhand dress. Mainly because it struck me as terrifically wasteful for such an important item to only enjoy one outing in its lifetime—but also because I fell in love with the swathes of crisp silk taffeta in my eighties frock. I quashed any squeamishness: even if the marriage of its former owner didn't end well, I'm sure it started with promise!

Wearing a vintage wedding dress isn't about frugality—although it certainly will save you a great deal of money. If you consider making the frock your 'something old', I guarantee you'll look unique, and far more original than every other bride who bought the latest trend that year. And the photos will be timeless.

If you're lucky enough to possess a tiny frame, you shouldn't have any trouble squeezing into bias-cut wedding frocks from the 1930s and 1940s—my favourite eras for modest, long-sleeved wedding attire. Bear in mind, many of the women who first wore them were teenagers or in their early twenties, so the sizes are not very forgiving for modern women, who tend to be married later in life.

Your frock of frocks need not be white or cream. Or any other neutral shade, come to think of it. It's your day, so if you fancy splashing out in Paula Yates red lace or Elsa Schiaparelli shocking pink, be my guest. But if your guests follow tradition, they won't be wearing white themselves, so you'll stand out in snowy tones. And if you can't be the centre of attention on your own wedding day, when can you? This is your time to shine.

Work in PROGRESS

A '50s lace wedding gown with stains and frayed hem. If rigorous cleaning fails, consider adding embellishment.

Beaded silk remnants salvaged from flea markets cover alice bands or damaged clutches for spectacular accessories.

A '70s addition to a '40s frock is unpicked and replaced. Stitch up a plunging neckline for ladylike chic, or add a demure panel.

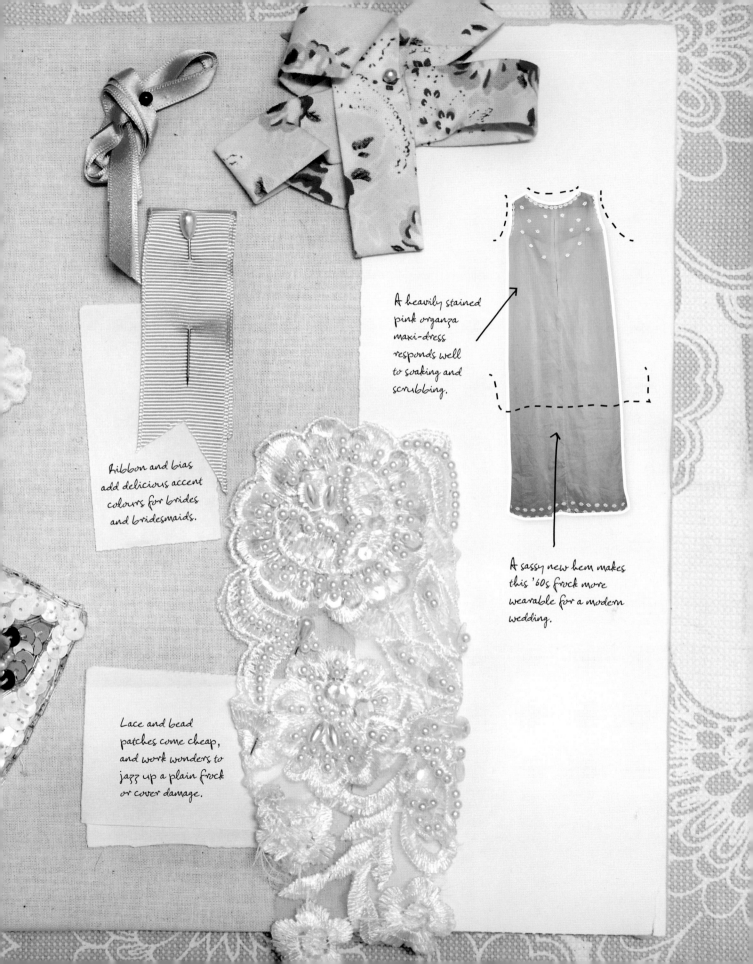

A heavily stained pink organza maxi-dress responds well to soaking and scrubbing.

Ribbon and bias add delicious accent colours for brides and bridesmaids.

A sassy new hem makes this '60s frock more wearable for a modern wedding.

Lace and bead patches come cheap, and work wonders to jazz up a plain frock or cover damage.

Wedding Belles

Here are just a few examples of vintage frocks I own which would make stunning and wonderfully original wedding dresses:

- a calf-length ivory brocade dress from the 1930s
- a high-necked, long-sleeved, bold-shouldered satin frock from the 1940s
- a pale lilac tulle-and-taffeta prom dress from the 1950s. This would also make a wonderful bridesmaid's dress for an extravagant or whimsical wedding party (dress 2, opposite)
- a spotted chiffon sundress from the 1950s, perfect for a hot climate, with a silk slip underneath (dress 3)
- a floor-length 1950s lace, tulle and silk scallop-necked frock (dress 4)
- a frilly, full-skirted number from the 1950s
- a long, beaded silver lamé Wiggle dress from the 1960s (dress 5).

I doubt any of them were made for a wedding in their time; I'd bet they were special frocks created for important events, such as debutante balls and elegant soirees—but that's what makes them such an original choice for a modern wedding.

Wear your vintage dress with pride, with a classic 'do and modern accessories for timeless chic, and put the money you've saved towards a fabulous honeymoon wardrobe instead—I did!

WEAR YOUR VINTAGE DRESS WITH PRIDE, WITH A CLASSIC 'DO AND MODERN ACCESSORIES FOR TIMELESS CHIC

You can't go past satin brocades for a special occasion. I adore this 1930s silk dress (on the far left). It's the perfect attire for a high-summer garden wedding.

The other four frocks would also make gorgeous modern wedding dresses.

Something old,
Something New

This floor-sweeping lacy frock was a beautifully made stage costume from the 1940s. I'm lucky enough to have an insight into its provenance, because I nabbed it myself from the archives of a renowned theatre outfitter's, at a one-off auction.

This dress had been altered so that the once-demure neckline became more plunging, and it had diamond-shaped sequinned beading added to its centre, which I thought looked a little cheap. From the diamond beading and low neckline, I'm guessing that it was updated during the 1970s. The metal zip placement at the side is just one of the indications of its vintage; even with the later adjustments, the original forties features shine through.

And, after some customisation, it's now perfect for another spell in the limelight.

CUSTOMISATION AND RESTORATION

A little grey from age, I gave the dress a good soaking in the bath with a wool wash, perfect for delicates. Without wringing, I laid it outside in the shade on a towel until it dried.

After removing the seventies embellishment, I added a beautiful sequin-and-bead silver leaf design, which is more in keeping with its 1940s roots. I also sewed up the neckline to mid-chest, hiding an over-enthusiastic cleavage for more ladylike bridal chic, and repaired a number of small tears in the lace skirt.

Tip: Many frocks are altered over the years to suit different owners and eras. It's common to find dresses with damaged or odd embellishment. Think beyond what's there to how you can change or remove the detailing for a vast, or even subtle, improvement.

Vintage *Wedding Accessories*

I've collected many special wedding items over the years, which I tend to give as gifts to girlfriends when they're getting married. White or silver beaded clutches from France and Hong Kong are a favourite gift for the woman who prefers a more modern look on her wedding day, but here are some other pieces you can weave into an otherwise on-trend bridal ensemble.

White beaded clutches are quite easy to find in flea markets and vintage stores—look out for one for yourself, or gift it to an engaged friend.

Classic wedding veils are beautiful, but not particularly popular at modern weddings. I prefer a headpiece such as this 1960s tulle and silk band, which looks elegant over a classic 'do.

This pretty fifties lace shrug is a lovely light cover-up for church weddings.

This stunning Guipure lace 1960s wedding coat is in immaculate condition and lined with a fine layer of tulle. A showstopper in itself, I would pair it with a very simple white shift, chic round-toed pumps, and a voluminous hair bun or French roll.

This sweet seventies chiffon-shouldered frock, first from the left, would be particularly fetching on a younger woman with a slim waist and no lumps and bumps. I love the flirty length and style, which would look great with heels and loose, long hair.

See the opposite page for details on the pink 60s frock shown here.

Prom dresses make truly fabulous wedding or bridesmaid dresses, even if they're a bit over-the-top for other occasions. This lilac lace and taffeta version (second from left) is a favourite. I wore it with a matching velvet cocktail hat, sweetheart-shaped apron, short beaded gloves and peep-toe heels to my girlfriend's baby shower. The theme? High Tea with a Twist, Alice in Wonderland-style. By the end of the long, hot day, I was barefoot, munching cupcakes on the lawn, while the sun set into the cocktail hour. It was a spectacular day.

This 1960s frock, second from the right, with delicate beading and diamantes, would be simply stunning on a pregnant bridesmaid, or work well for those with a thicker waist. I'm bowled over by the detail in this dress—especially the expensive silk organza lining, which you can't really see but feels deliciously feather-light against the skin.

Demure, full-skirted fifties styles suit women of all ages. I adore this calf-length couture lace, tulle and satin frock, pictured on the far right. It would look beautiful with a simple bouquet of roses, lavender or hydrangeas. It also makes a statement mother-of-the-bride frock, paired with a chic little cocktail hat or embellished head piece.

Chic Bridesmaids

It's amazing how anguished brides can become about how their wedding party is dressed—surely there's enough to worry about already? Apparently not, as I've known countless women who have agonised over the bridesmaids' dress decision.

I've been a bridesmaid twice, and both times my girlfriends were kind enough to allow me to wear whatever I fancied, so I consider myself lucky. For my own wedding, I told my four bridesmaids they could do the same, but they actually decided to coordinate what they were wearing. Considering they were on different continents at the time, the girls made a good attempt at matching, in the bold fuchsia accent colour I'd chosen for our theme. They looked gorgeous in their chosen frocks, opting for a range of styles which complemented each other uniquely.

I think it's important for women to wear a style they prefer when they're a bridesmaid, simply because all women are different, and it's rare indeed if everyone can look great in the same dress (unless you're more restrained than me, and only have one bridesmaid). Plus, it's good to see people looking happy and comfortable in what they're wearing, and that's hard to do when you're standing next to someone in the same dress (John Donne was right: comparisons *are* odious).

Here are a few vintage frocks which would make simply beautiful bridesmaids' dresses. Most of the styles are a bit frou-frou for everyday wear, but at a wedding each of them would really shine. I've chosen five frocks in similar tones to show how each could be worn by different-shaped women at the same wedding party.

FAIRGROUND FLOSS BRIDESMAID'S DRESS

There's a time and a place for Twiggy-style sixties cuteness … and what better place than a tropical summer wedding?

Ordinarily, I think it's a shame when stunning floor-length frocks are permanently chopped off in the interests of making them more wearable (although, of course it's better to get *some* use out of them). This dress (second from left, opposite) is an exception: simply too, too much in its original guise, this 1960s daisy-dotted organza number with matching taffeta shift looks amazing now it's shortened to a flattering above-the-knee length. It would make a beautiful wedding-party dress, particularly for any bridesmaid with a baby bump (is it just me, or do many people decide to get married during their friends' pregnancies?).

CUSTOMISATION

This dress was a real mess when I found it, which is why it only cost a few dollars. I diligently soaked and scrubbed over a series of days to remove yellow stains and grey marks from its outer organza layer before attempting to customise it. Finally, she came up good as new.

Using a quilter's cutting pad, ruler and rolling blade, I cut each layer of this frock separately, making sure the organza outer was slightly longer than the shift. With each one, I rolled the raw edge under and machine-sewed in a straight line, to avoid frayed edges.

*A typical floral silk thirties evening gown
with brooch and matching lace jacket.*

*Dusky pink pin-tucked and zip-fronted
thirties day dress.*

CLASSIC  *Thirties*

Heavily influenced by the rise of Hollywood and silver-screen style, the 1930s saw a return to polished elegance and softer, prettier styles. Dresses and gowns of the era boasted lower to full-length hemlines, with shoulder pads and practical full sleeves. Clothing was less restrictive or reliant upon figure-shaping corsets, and bias-cut satin evening dresses (which hugged every curve of a woman's body) were de rigueur. In juxtaposition, the pared-back simplicity of daywear reflected the financial strife and lean years of the Great Depression.

Designer Madeleine Vionnet, said to be the creator of the bias cut and the cowl, championed a new silhouette by creating silk gowns with plunging backs and halter necks which were also heavily adorned with sequins, beads and ruffles. But overall, form was the focus. Heavily draped gowns were accessorised with fur for both day and night-time wear, if one was wealthy enough to indulge in the latest, opulent fashions.

A jabot frill at the neckline was a common decorative element of thirties garments, and dresses sported high waists, bows, flounces, and strong or oversized shoulders and sleeves with Art Deco references in either their pattern or design elements. Day dresses were usually made from crepe or cotton, and while designer Elsa Schiaparelli played with zippers in fashion, they were not commonly used on clothing until the 1940s. As such, most 1930s garments were either button-down or fastened with press-studs at the side and back of the collar.

It is rare to find many fashions of the thirties intact, because rationing during the following decade was so severe that recycling fabrics and making do with what you already owned was a fact of life. Thus, 1930s knitwear in particular was unravelled and re-used during the war effort to make soldier's socks, blankets, and other utilitarian items.

WORK THE LOOK

Necklines and hemlines for thirties day dresses were modest by today's standards. Paired with long sleeves, the look was demure, with individual flair focused on tailoring, neat shoulder padding and pin-tucks, piping and pleating details.

Raise hemlines on sleeves and skirts for more modern style by folding under and ironing flat before sewing into place. For sleeves, you might need to unpick the inside seam before you do so for a looser fit. To expose more décolletage, unpick the seam commonly running down the middle of the bust, and fold back at the collar to create a more daring V-shape, sewn into place by hand. With a camisole or lacy slip worn underneath, a deep V with such precise thirties tailoring will look superb.

Pair with a belt at the waist and long leather boots for a more bohemian look, or neat round-toed heels, a dashing brooch and velvet bolero for evening.

Thirties evening wear in silk, satin or taffeta may be riddled with moth holes—use iron-on bonding to repair, along with fabric stolen from the hem and hand-stitched around the diameter for extra strength, or cut away a terribly damaged base to create a shorter dress. There is always the option of replacing the lower skirt with matching fabric in a high-contrast design; this looks particularly fetching when added on a diagonal line to emphasize the bias cut.

Cover stains with beaded appliqué or bows and pleats fashioned from hem fabric: given that items were made by hand and expected to be pressed into many years of service by the wearer, excess fabric was often left in the seams and hemlines for later alterations.

Gorgeous
JACKETS &
COATS

A FABULOUS JACKET OR COAT CAN BE WORN ON TOP OF anything for warmth, chic-ness and to finish off a look. I'm all for the ease of throwing on a frock and heading out the door, but when the occasion or temperature calls for more, a coordinated jacket or coat can pull together an ensemble and make you feel supremely polished. And good jackets are the workhorses of your wardrobe; chosen well, they should last you for many seasons, and sometimes a lifetime.

The right style also hides a thousand sins … it may even become your 'signature'; think of the recently departed editor of French *Vogue*, Carine Roitfeld, and her vast collection of trench coats and Chanel jackets.

I love the drama of a spectacular bolero or proper dress coat, particularly when I'm feeling the need to hide the fact I've had one too many macarons. That's when I pair something bright and eye-catching up top with a simple, dark frock or separates beneath for a miraculously slimming effect.

These are my key styles for when I'm feeling glam, bohemian, or in need of comfort. Some I'll wear just to accentuate the charm of judicious layering, such as the linen shrug. All of these pieces should be easy to find (and customise). Add them to your arsenal of killer looks for an alternative take on the classic staples.

Work in
PROGRESS

Bored with beige? Zest up tired pieces with eye-popping dyes in ultraviolet, fuscia or tangerine.

When intricate repair stitching fails, 100% cotton lace covers tears in this bed jacket turned shrug.

This is one of my 'museum' pieces, sadly she is too small to fit anyone other than a child.

A lovely yet damaged silk velvet number from the '30s comes alive with purple bias and silk lining.

Bye-bye Burberry check, hello silk lining. Shiny red buttons replace boring beige.

Feathers fantastic: add drama and glamour with a strip of green-black plumage.

As you can see from the before photos, it was quite long to begin with. But my now-shortie kimono works so well as an open overcoat or jacket.

An authentically faded '70s Wrangler jacket loves a little Liberty reinvention. Brit-tastic.

Once-were-Victorians
Linen Shrug

Queen Victoria's reign (1837–1901) marked prosperity for the United Kingdom, as profits from the flourishing British colonies flowed back to the Empire and allowed improvements to be made within people's homes and in industry.

My home is Victorian; my husband and I are fans of the soaring spaces, plaster ceiling roses, ornate arches and other architectural features of the era, which celebrate function with dashingly elegant form. The Victorian fashions were beautiful, too (if a little on the restrictive side).

Many moons ago I found this dainty linen piece—a wisp of a thing—in a flea market. I'm fairly certain it was once an undergarment of some sort, or perhaps a bed jacket. Yellowing, and with its hand-wrought lace bodice shredded to bits through age and lack of care, I tenderly brought it back to life through meticulous soaking and repair.

Even though this linen lovely is one of my rare 'museum pieces', she is perfectly wearable on a day-to-day basis as a bolero or shrug; indeed I wear her often—layering over a tank top with jeans and lots of jewellery, or over a short frock. Although it's too small on me to do up, it looks perfectly pretty worn undone … unlike my delectable Victorian-era silk jacket, which is just for show (and too tiny to fit anyone other than a nine-year-old).

I TENDERLY BROUGHT BACK TO LIFE ITS HAND-WROUGHT LACE BODICE, SHREDDED TO BITS THROUGH AGE AND LACK OF CARE

Customisation

First, I removed the simple, superfluous mother-of-pearl buttons, and then carefully soaked this piece in a bucket of nappy cleaning solution. I bought a length of matching cotton lace trim from a haberdashery, and pinned it carefully to the shredded lace bodice in concentric half-circles, where the edges of the lace bodice were most damaged. I then stitched it on with the machine in layers.

A few small steps for a very big difference, and it's made the collar more hardy—hardy enough to last another one hundred-plus years, perhaps.

Better than bed
Jacket

The concept of a bed jacket is so quaint, and just a little saucy, don't you think? I always think they're a bit 'come in to my boudoir …' Too gorgeous for the bedroom alone, I've been wearing circa 1960s versions as light, open overcoats for years now—usually over a short, fitted frock for a touch of delicate glamour. They also look great belted over a satin slip as a sort of coat-dress.

RAVEN BEAUTY

This black lace bed jacket with ruffled sleeves is very Dolce & Gabbana, and reminds me of the label's campaign featuring Madonna in Italy. Boasting a flair for the dramatic with newly added feathers, she never ceases to draw attention. She's my favourite companion for a night on the town over bold colours such as scarlet, chartreuse or rose-coloured satin.

CUSTOMISATION

When I bought this jacket, the lace was brittle and torn in a number of places, and faded to light orange-brown from sun exposure. I restored it to a deep jet black with dye, and added a collar of dark emerald feathers by hand with small, firm stitches. I also repaired as much of the lace as I could by hand. I considered taking it to the Lace Guild for expert repair, but decided against it; it's still shredded in places, but in a way that looks deliberate and beautiful, rather than shoddy.

Tip: My vintage dealer friend, Jessica Guthrie, passed on this invaluable cleaning tip: for clothes with extensive yellowing and particularly stubborn rust stains, dissolve a capful of nappy soaking powder in a bowl filled with very hot water, and stir until fully dissolved. Pour the bowl into a bathtub, adding more hot water (or warm water, if your item is anything other than cotton or linen) and lay your item or items in the solution so they are covered. Leave to soak for a few hours, then hang on a washing line or lay out in full sunlight, without rinsing out the cleaning solution. Watch the stains disappear, then finish with rinsing and a final dry. It only works with lots of sunlight; something to do with enzymes reacting to sun exposure—it's like magic!

Speed-dial
Tokyo Kimonos

The first time I went to Japan, I visited a nightclub in Tokyo's notorious Roppongi district, and got the shock of my life to see young Japanese hipsters getting down to the music in full traditional regalia— men and women alike. Think kimonos, wooden sandals, white socks and elaborate hairdos ... and they seemed right at home amid the indigo denim, spiky hair, hoodies and streetwear sported by the other patrons. I'd assumed the kimono's popularity was a thing of the past, but apparently traditional dress was enjoying a revival that year. It made me want to don one myself and make use of those dramatic sleeves in a heady disco swirl!

Confession: I *love* kimonos, and often swan about the house wearing one as a dressing gown, feeling very *Madame Butterfly*. But they're too beautiful for my eyes only. That's why I modify them to make them more practical (so it doesn't look like I've stepped out in public wearing my jim-jams). I currently have four, and perhaps don't wear them nearly enough, although I display one by hanging it from a picture rail—indeed, the detail in the fabric and hand-stitched seams *are* a work of art.

This delicate pink silk version on the far right is one of a cache of stunning 1960s kimonos I bought from a woman selling off her sizeable collection (more than two hundred kimonos, apparently!). As you can see from the 'before' photos, it was quite long to begin with. But my now-shortie kimono works so well as an open overcoat or jacket, and is particularly cool when cinched with this braided seventies belt in place of an obi.

> KIMONOS, WOODEN SANDALS, WHITE TOED SOCKS AND ELABORATE HAIRDOS ... SEEMED RIGHT AT HOME AMIDST ALL THE INDIGO DENIM, SPIKY HAIR, HOODIES AND STREETWEAR

Two Japanese kimono styles which make a dramatic entrance when worn as a jacket (the black, red and gold satin) and dress (the purple silk) respectively. Both items needed minor repairs to the torn silk and gaping seams, but my handiwork is virtually invisible, with the help of iron-on bonding and small, careful stitches.

CUSTOMISATION

I tried on my kimono and worked out how long it needed to be to cover my behind—a short kimono is the ticket for those days when you want to draw attention away from your figure (wear it over a slimming black frock or separates)—then I popped a pin in that spot.

Laying the kimono on a flat surface, I cut from one lapel at a downward angle, levelling out once I reached the side seam. I then cut halfway across the back, freehand, in a straight line. When I reached the halfway mark, I folded the kimono over, carefully matching up the seams to make sure they were level on each side, and using the side I'd cut as a pattern to do the rest.

Then, I put aside the excess fabric for later (kimono silk is divine for lining things and creating all manner of accessories … see page 59 for the 'Yo-Yos', created from the remnants to adorn a 1930s slip) and tied knots in all the newly cut threads. Kimonos are generally hand-stitched, so if you cut a thread it's likely to work its way loose until your kimono starts falling apart—make sure you tie off those ends. Then I cut away the excess fabric inside the layers, to make it easier to machine-sew.

I'm all for copying the techniques used by the person who made the garment—the consistency makes your adjustments look professional and less like a DIY project. (Be dictated by the style as well as the technique of the original garment.) But, when it came to this kimono, I thought a stitched hem on the bottom would look quite nice as a form of binding on the inside lining. So I machine-stitched it across, raw edge rolled under, unravelling the lapels to ensure the line of stitching would be invisible when folded inside. I then ironed the hem flat, and hand-stitched the lapels back in place, and firmly together.

Tip: When customising an item, study and emulate the techniques used by the garment's original maker, rather than adding new ones—this looks more professional. Take note of techniques such as certain stitches, stitch length, seam style and embellishment, just to name a few. You might learn a thing or two, and it will help improve your sewing skills overall.

London calling
Denim Jacket

This rebellious little number reminds me of legendary British band The Clash's punky classic, 'London Calling'. Indeed, I feel a bit edgy myself when I step out in it, even if a real punk would eat me alive for suggesting it.

I've taken an old Wrangler denim jacket—an original from the seventies, complete with bleach fading, and purchased for a few dollars at a flea market—and added strips of Liberty print for a Union Jack-style fix. It's an irreverent, timeless piece that dresses down the most serious outfit.

Most of all, I love how it seems to go with everything: my favourite outfit sees it downplay a bodycon dress with flats and footless tights. It also looks magic with a chignon and floor-sweeping evening gown (believe it or not); over a satin slip or cotton summer frock, matched with sandals and with tousled hair tumbling down; or with a pair of high-waisted indigo palazzo pants, cotton tank and towering wedges, hair pulled into a slick, high pony.

CUSTOMISATION

Firstly, lay out your denim jacket on a flat surface, with the back facing up, then place the strips in the rough Union Jack formation before pinning in place. Sew together with your machine on a tight zig-zag stitch, reversing a few times at either end for strength. Yep, it's that simple. You might even want to leave some of the threads trailing rather than snipping them off for unravelled-looking charm.

You will need:

- a beaten-up vintage denim jacket. Go for as tight and short as you feel comfortable in: it will look snappier than a loose-fitting version
- strips of blue, red and white-toned Liberty print, or simple blue, red and white cotton for a more traditional Union Jack
- pins
- sewing machine and thread.

Beam me up, Scotty Trench

The rakish trench, a modern wardrobe staple, is actually so-called because it was designed for soldiers to wear in the grim conditions of battlefield trenches during World War One. Not only is it hardy—made from a thick cotton drill or gabardine—but it can be dressed up or down, works well year-round, doubles as a raincoat and can even be worn on its own with little more than a slip underneath. Wear the belt knotted, rather than buckled: it's all about insouciant elegance.

Christopher Bailey's gloriously twisted designs for Burberry Prorsum may reign as the style *du jour*, but there's no reason not to consider recycling an older version of the classic Burberry trench coat for a more economical fashion fix.

I was given this much-loved Burberry trench by my friend Shauna, but the lining had been darned too many times to mention and was looking tired after thirty-plus years of hard service. The first step was to take it to a specialist dry-cleaner to eliminate stubborn marks and signs of damage. Then, it was on to updating it with a new lining. I've used silk in an original design, purchased for a steal at an end-of-season sale from Australian design duo Ginger & Smart. I've also added new red buttons in a delicious shade of raspberry and given it a slicker, much shorter length.

Eat your heart out, Humphrey Bogart … This is definitely the beginning of a beautiful friendship.

CONSIDER RECYCLING AN OLDER VERSION OF THE CLASSIC BURBERRY TRENCH COAT FOR A MORE ECONOMICAL FASHION FIX

You will need:

- a trench coat
- approximately two metres of lining fabric in a contrasting design—go wild—100 per cent silk or cotton works best
- Quick Unpick or seam ripper
- pins
- dressmaker's scissors
- sewing machine
- beige cotton thread
- buttons (ten or so)
- hand needle
- cotton thread to match buttons.

CUSTOMISATION

1. Use your seam ripper to unpick Burberry's signature checked lining, then unpick the label and place aside. You might want to cut the lining from the coat with your scissors instead, which is fine as long as you snip as close to the seams as possible, without chopping into the coat. If possible, preserve each piece of lining in its original shape (the reason for this is given below).

2. Try on your trench in front of a mirror, and decide on a new length. Adjust the pins until you're happy with the result. If your new length varies only slightly, you could simply fold the excess fabric over and stitch in place, in case you want to take it down later. If there's quite a bit of excess, chop it off (as I've done), but leave at least a few centimetres for seam allowance. Fold the raw edge under and stitch along the hemline with your beige thread.

3. Lay out the old lining to get an idea of the measurements for the new one—and cut out the shape using the Burberry check as your pattern. I unpicked the old lining to the three pieces originally used, cutting my new silk lining from these patterns (this is the easiest way to replace a tired lining—and why it's better to preserve the old lining when removing). I also left a seam allowance on each side. Fold the raw edge of the bottom hem under, and stitch in a straight line.

4. Turn the trench coat inside out and pin the lining to the inside. If your sleeves are lined with silk which is still in good condition, stitch the main lining to the sleeve lining around the armholes. Machine-sew the rest of the lining to the interior of the coat, making sure there's no tension in the thread to pull the lining out of shape. If you're having trouble getting your machine to sew around all the tricky corners, use your needle and thread to stitch difficult areas into place.

5. There's nothing wrong with being proud of the provenance—if you love its design pedigree, pin the Burberry label back in place and stitch it to the lining, either with the machine or by hand.

6. Attach the bottom hem of the lining to the coat with a few small stitches—*only* at each vertical seam. This will ensure your lining sits flat, but doesn't pull or restrict movement.

7. Unpick all the buttons and sew on your new ones with matching thread. Here I've removed ten large, and four small, ones; I added buttons in a lovely contrasting shade of red. This is spy style at its best!

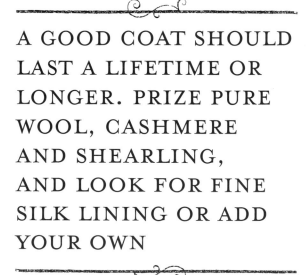

A GOOD COAT SHOULD
LAST A LIFETIME OR
LONGER. PRIZE PURE
WOOL, CASHMERE
AND SHEARLING,
AND LOOK FOR FINE
SILK LINING OR ADD
YOUR OWN

Volare
Bolero

Dean Martin sang of it: 'volare' is from the Italian verb 'to fly', and that's the feeling this dusky ottoman bolero instils in me when I wear it. I imagine it once matched a late 1940s/early 1950s ball gown in the same fabric. Maybe that's why I feel so much lighter on my feet when I wear it—the former occupant's toes barely touched the floor as she waltzed over polished dance floors ...

CUSTOMISATION

When found at a flea market, my bolero was quite plain, inexpensive and faded at the cuffs, which I rolled up and sewed under. I invested a pretty penny embellishing over areas of damage and around the collar, but it was well worth it for this spectacular evening cover-up. The beading was purchased in a strip from a luxury fabric store and stitched on by hand.

Tip: Invest in superb-quality embellishments for well-structured, but otherwise plain, vintage pieces—you'll be amazed how expensive it can make them look. The blend of couture tailoring with custom-chosen elements will make you feel a million bucks.

Feeling natty
Wool Jacket

This beautifully cut, double-breasted houndstooth jacket from the 1950s or 1960s has been in my wardrobe for years. I used to wear it to work over a pencil skirt, in winter, with a separate collar of fur; it was always chic and useful—a real workhorse of my wardrobe. The beige and grey tones seemed to complement anything, but it lacked a little in personality.

When I realised I hadn't worn my jacket in years (and it'd been taking up valuable wardrobe space), I considered passing it on. I then came to the conclusion I was simply tired of the muted tones, which reminded me of schlepping back and forth to a sensible job in an office. I wanted to give it a zingy lift, and a new lease of life: a makeover to suit my current lifestyle, and prevent me from (inevitably) buying another piece to fill its place. I think the transformation worked: the colour stands out in a crowd, and garners lovely compliments from people admiring the unusual shade.

And if I ever go back to that conservative job, I can always dye it black!

CUSTOMISATION

I removed the boring plastic buttons, and decided upon a new colour: ultra violet. I liked the idea of a pretty blue, but worried that the original beige and grey might make the blue turn out an unattractive murky green. This lavender shade was perfect, with the beige undertones giving it a warmer hue than if it were covering only the ivory.

Wearing a sturdy pair of gloves, I stirred the concoction for half an hour, making sure the dye thoroughly covered the wool (which, like silk, always takes dye less well than other fabrics). You can see from the lining that the outer is more faded than it could have been—a look I was going for.

After rinsing out the dye until the water ran clear, and drying it in the shade, I ironed the jacket and stitched on a new set of vintage buttons, which have much more personality than the previous set.

Tips:

- *When a style goes out of fashion and then comes in again, it generally becomes a 'classic'—that's why you can wear your cropped tux for years to come (and not feel a fashion tragic).*

- *Look out for military jackets that fit you, or look outsized in a charming way. If buttons are missing, try replacing them with real metal buttons, even if you can't find the original military-issue on eBay or at markets (plastic looks cheap). And don't be confined to khaki: I'm still looking for a red-wool uniform jacket I can give this treatment to.*

Totally biased
Velvet Blazer

THESE GARMENTS ARE GOING TO BE INCREDIBLY RARE ONE DAY … THE CUT OF THIS JACKET IS SO FINE, IT SHOULD BE IN A MUSEUM

I can't tell you how much I love velvet—particularly silk velvet, which is what this jacket happens to be. There's something about the fabric when it's old and worn that I just can't go past. Proper vintage velvet reminds me of the childhood story of the Velveteen Rabbit. Threadbare, but soft as fur, old velvet can be deliciously charming. I love that crushed look it gets when the pile's rubbed the wrong way—in fact, I think I far prefer it to the newer, thicker kind. And when I do buy new velvet, I always aspire for it to acquire that vintage look and feel. I can't help rubbing my fingers against it when I wear it (which must make me appear a bit strange at times).

This jacket is one of the most inexpensive pieces I own, but its pedigree is unmistakeable. It's pure 1930s, and so fitted it had to have been made especially for the owner who, thankfully, was exactly my size. I found it at my local flea market.

The stall-holders—a mother and daughter—were obviously clearing out their closets. They seemed less concerned with making a profit than soaking up the beautiful early autumn sun over takeaway coffees, and spending some time together. We chatted amiably as I flicked through the jumbled items on their table and single rack of clothes. The fare was mostly standard chainstore seconds, until I came upon this one piece. Frayed around the edges and with both sleeves hanging on by loose threads, its matching black lining had come away almost entirely. I asked how much they were willing to sell it for. 'Four dollars,' was the reply. I was so excited, my hands shook when I extracted the coins from my purse. 'Thank you so much,' I said. 'It's beautiful. Can I ask why you're getting rid of it?' The daughter, who must have been about my age, told me with a smile: 'I'm just sick of it. It's been hanging in my wardrobe forever.'

I understand the sentiment. It gets to a point when you've had something for so long that you fail to 'see' it. And as so few of us have the storage—or desire—to squirrel everything away, on the off-chance we might rediscover our love for it again, it seems sensible to pass things on. But I don't think I could have parted with this. When I'm done, my lovely jacket is going in a box for my daughter. Because these garments are going to be so rare one day, and the cut of this jacket is so fine, it should be in a museum. Let's hope my daughter values it as much as I do.

CUSTOMISATION

The fit of this jacket was absolutely perfect when I found it, so it didn't need taking in or shortening. But the lining was trashed, and the thread in almost every single seam was disintegrating. The very same day I bought it, I found some paisley silk in a basket of jumbled scarves. It set me back fifty cents. When I got home, I cut away the old jacket lining and went over every line of stitching on my sewing machine. Then I hand-stitched the sleeve cuffs back into place (they were hanging down over the wrists), and removed the four sets of press-studs on the cuffs, because they felt just that bit too tight when done up (and looked less than smart when undone).

Next, I laid the jacket on a flat surface and cut the silk scarf to the shape of the jacket's inside back (leaving a seam allowance around the edges). I stitched the paisley in by hand, then went over some of the seams with my sewing machine. I adore a contrasting silk lining—the designer Paul Smith often adds this to his jackets and coats, and I think it's such a jaunty touch.

The last step was finding the right binding to cover the damaged edges of the collar and lapels. Not only were they frayed, but also showing age discolouration. I didn't want to lose the vintage feel of the jacket, but knew it needed something to smarten it up. I found a perfect satin binding in a rich shade of purple, which picks out the colours in the silk lining. I machine-stitched it the entire way around, on its outside edge, then folded the binding over and hand-stitched it in place on the inside. I found that the extra layers of fabric around the edge have the advantage of stiffening the collar and lapels. I love it.

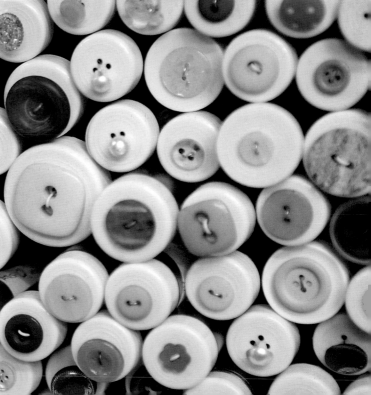

Dusky-pink bias-cut crepe evening
dress, with silver beading at its waist.
The boxy shoulders of wartime are
highlighted in this common design.

Cotton floral print dress with
scalloped neckline for day wear.

CLASSIC *Forties*

Forties fashion was more austere and constrained, due to the climate of World War Two. Heavy rations were imposed and women had to think creatively to 'make do and mend'. Colours were usually sombre in black, navy, forest green and muted dusty shades, cut in a narrow, boxy silhouette which saved on material and referenced military clothing worn the world over.

Just as with food rationing during the war, clothing could also only be purchased with coupons from 1941 onwards. CC41 (Clothing Control 1941) is the now-collectable label from the forties, and clothing bearing this label was required to be of a certain standard and quality, with no unnecessary trims and the dictated fabric allowances in each garment adhered to—such was the severity of the rationing system during this period. It wasn't until 1947, when Dior's New Look came in, that colour, frivolity and fabric yardage was again celebrated in fashion.

Designers and the home seamstress had to think creatively during wartime; as a result, many intriguing patterns came out of the era. Due to fabric shortages, sequins and embroidery were often used to adorn evening wear and embellish garments, and beautiful buttons were used as a statement (but only when necessary). Crepe and rayon were the most commonly used fabrics, with silk used sparingly, to save on costs. Novelty prints were also popular, and showed patriotism through their designs with flag, map and compass motifs.

WORK THE LOOK

Similar to the 1930s, demure hems, sleeves and necklines can be easily readjusted for a more modern look. Beaded crepe dresses with strong shoulders are an outstanding fashion staple of the era, but crepe-and-wool skirt suits were also very popular, taking the lead from men's military attire. Separate a jacket from its skirt to wear over a T-shirt or blouse with denim, or leave undone and layered over a short floral frock in cotton or silk, referencing the Queen at Balmoral when you do. A well-tailored forties suit still looks magic in a modern-day office environment.

Mend damage by matching beads and filling in any missing areas of embellishment, and decorate over holes with embroidery or beading. Use iron-on bonding, along with fabric taken from the hem and hand-stitched into place, to cover up large tears, holes or stains, and cover fraying hems or collars with satin bias-binding.

Some of my favourite items from this era are the hats: styles were compact and simple, military in flavour, or infused with intricate details to make up for material shortages. They perfectly complement the spare design of the clothing. I have quite a collection, but rarely find the opportunity to wear them: hat-wearers are a particularly intrepid brand of fashionista in this day and age!

Too-chic
TOPS &
BLOUSES

WATCH OUT FOR THE BLOUSE COMEBACK! FROCKS FROM bygone eras grab most of the attention, yes, but an unusual vintage top or blouse can add understated glamour to any casual ensemble, becoming the whimsical focus of an otherwise rudimentary outfit. They're great for days when you're not really in the mood for working a vintage look (pair with denim jeans or a simple black skirt for off-duty charm) and are more adaptable than almost any other item for dressing up or down, depending on the occasion. A high-collared sixties organza number with pleated frills, paired with a gorgeous bra and some dashing palazzo pants, is somehow smarter than a dress on certain occasions, and will ensure you stand out from the crowd.

I love how a blah day can be improved with a sparkly top or the demure charms of a crisp, white linen blouse, which makes me feel spring-fresh, no matter what the season. I adore the rock-chick charms of a trashed band T-shirt, or old men's work shirts worn oversized with the sleeves rolled up; and how a figure-hugging bodysuit is guaranteed to make you feel all slinky and fabulous on thin days, without worrying you've gone overboard in a head-to-toe Alaïa moment.

Prim silk blouses, bodycon bodysuits, crisp white linen and traditional Breton stripes with a twist … just a few of my favourites for adorning the top half when opting for separates. Here are some pieces that will always remain centre of attention in any get-up, and a few hints and tips for embellishing and distressing to achieve the best look. Make one item the focus of your outfit, or be bold and turn up the volume with clashing colours, stripes and checks: the choice is yours.

Work in PRO·GRESS

Be bold: bright dyes look sensational on crushed, dusty silks and give a spectacular makeover.

DYLON
13
CARNIVAL

A nude girdle becomes a fab bodysuit with dye, new cups and this lovely bead & sequin heart.

Sometimes, more is more. Add ribbon or beaded trim to a plain hem or neckline for a charming, designer-style reinvention.

A peasant blouse looks gorgeous with added tassels. I made these myself with glass beads, metallic and embroidery thread.

Create drama with feathered epaulettes, made by attaching rows of feathers to a pair of plain black shoulder pads with needle and thread. Secure to a favourite blouse or jacket with safety pins or strips of adhesive velcro.

Collect all sorts of transforming embellishments in the form of these fab beaded patches and shiny sequins.

Wings of Desire Bodysuit

As a young girl, I often had romantic notions about running away with the circus to become a trapeze artist. Perhaps adventure stories with plucky heroines planted the seed? The kind of fiercely independent girl-women who never said no to attempting a death-defying feat or three.

Then I watched Wim Wenders' poignant, evocative film, *Wings of Desire,* as a teenager. Set in a war-tortured Berlin where trench-coat-wearing angels follow the thoughts of the living inhabitants, the angel Damiel forsakes the beauty of the clouds for a mesmerising, melancholic trapeze artist. Marion (that lovely circus performer, played by actress Solveig Dommartin) was the embodiment of all my childhood dreams. I'm still trying to capture her sparkly carnival style all these years later.

Pair this bodysuit with a pair of jeans and beaded cardigan for an everyday dream come true, or with a crushed tulle tutu if you're feeling whimsical, wild and brave.

CUSTOMISATION

I usually draw the line at buying intimate vintage scanties, but I could tell this fifties Playtex undergarment had never been worn when I bought it for a few dollars at a flea market. Originally a nude colour I'm not particularly fond of (even in underwear), I dyed it royal blue along with a number of other items. Whereas the other pieces turned out a deep hue, I chanced my luck that it would come up pale, given it's mostly synthetic. I love the washed-out colour, which strikes me as suitably dreamy for its purpose as a bodysuit.

This underwear was initially worn with a 1950s-style bullet bra or stiff cups, but I've added soft-form cups instead. Adjustable straps means there's more than enough support, and the *pièce de résistance* is a pre-bought sequin and bead heart stitched to the front.

Tip: *If you love this piece but feel squeamish about purchasing secondhand undergarments, buy a modern version (generally inexpensive and easy to find in department and lingerie stores) and dye it before adding favoured embellishments.*

Butter wouldn't melt
French Blouse

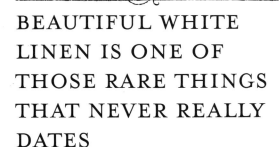

BEAUTIFUL WHITE LINEN IS ONE OF THOSE RARE THINGS THAT NEVER REALLY DATES

This antique sleeveless blouse was created as underwear to be worn beneath prim Victorian-era layers. Imagine what a proper lady from those times would make of seeing me out in public wearing it—no doubt she would think me a lady of the night! But beautiful white linen is one of those rare things that never really dates. And, fitted as this style is, it looks lovely worn simply with a skirt or pair of jeans, or under a beaded cashmere cardigan.

I found this top while fossicking through a basket of unwanted clothes in a dusty French *brocante*, in full bowerbird mode. It was age-stained, holey and missing buttons. All it needed was some patient TLC. Enter: me.

CUSTOMISATION

The trouble with properly antique items is damage through use, moths and sheer age—this top is more than a century old, after all. Just think of what it's seen over the years, and how the world has changed since its creation.

I soaked it overnight in a nappy cleaning solution, then hung it out in the sunshine, without rinsing. The age stains disappeared within a few hours. I then took to it with pure white thread, invisibly mending the moth holes and tears. I also replaced its missing buttons with a new-old set, found at a flea market.

Tip: If you're unsure about how to mend an antique piece, look closely to see if there have been any repairs already—chances are, you'll find them. Clothes were too precious way back when to throw away when they started to show signs of age, and earlier eras of women were the masters of darning, bringing damaged linens and clothing back to life. Copy the mending styles of such vintage pieces for an authentic feel. This might mean carrying out repairs by hand, rather than on the machine. But this is one area where a little patience goes a long way.

Chinois silk  Blouses

INDULGE IN THE DELECTABLE DELIGHTS OF LIGHTWEIGHT SILK AGAINST BARE SKIN

Prettily embroidered silk blouses were one of my first fashion fixations. As a child, my parents would take my brothers and me to Chinatown for special-occasion dinners. As a treat, we were allowed to buy something beforehand from one of the dusty shops overflowing with thrillingly foreign-looking imported goods. Once, I chose a delicate paper and wood parasol printed with flowers, birds and indecipherable Chinese script, which I broke and cried over for days. Another time, a pair of velvet slippers in a rich burgundy, boasting beautiful beaded butterflies (try saying that quickly) ... And, most memorably, I fell head-over-heels in love with a dusky blue silk blouse which I simply wore to death before I grew too big and it literally ripped apart at the seams.

As a teenager, I sought out the same silk blouses, and have been wearing them ever since.

You can still buy the same styles I wore as a child; even when new, the look and feel is pure nostalgia. One or two properly old versions are lurking in my wardrobe, waiting to be paired with jeans for a relaxed off-duty look, or tucked into a sharp pin skirt or pleated trousers for an important meeting. And I have a couple of new ones, too.

Chinois silk blouses come in a wide range of styles, both short- and long-sleeved. Find one which suits you—I prefer lapels or ruffles to the traditional Chinese collar, for example—and indulge in the delectable delights of lightweight silk against bare skin.

Customisation

The most difficult thing can be finding one of these blouses in a suitable colour—sweet-tooth pastels aren't for everyone. Dye by hand to achieve the exact hue you're looking for.

Chinese silk blouses are also quite boxy, traditionally. Try a few darts in the back, or tailoring the side seams for a fitted look, as I've done with the grey blouse shown here. This works a charm to flatter your figure, and feels more couture than Chinatown.

Tip: For gridlocked metal zippers, rub an ordinary taper candle on the outside of the zipper teeth and gently try moving it again. This ingenious trick has saved me from throwing the baby out with the bathwater on numerous occasions. When the fabric's trapped, take a few deep breaths and try to work it out calmly, or ask for help if you're impatient—frantic tearing now will only lead to tears later.

Slinky Smock

THE APPEAL OF A FLATTERING, WELL-MADE BLOUSE NEVER DATES

This pretty sixties or seventies georgette smock by obscure designer Foulke & Foulke New York, is one beautiful blouse, destined to be treasured. You can tell it's been made with love: why bother covering the stainless steel press-studs with tiny strips of fabric and hand-stitching, if not? Or backing tissue-weight fabric with an immaculately sewn silk lining? I haven't found any other rare pieces by the same designer in my travels, apart from on eBay searches, but those that have survived look lovely. They appear to have specialised in those matching jacket/dress combos which were so popular back then, thanks to Jackie Kennedy, pre-Onassis.

The appeal of a flattering, well-made blouse never dates. I love the floaty georgette and perfect-weight sleeves of this top, which fall loosely in a willowy way around the wrists, making them look all thin and elegant. Such is the power of a good smock.

I was forced to replace the metal zipper when it refused to budge one evening after a wonderful night out. I eventually emerged, very red-faced after a lot of huffing and puffing, but I'd damaged the teeth too much with frantic pulling for it to ever close smoothly again.

RESTORATION

Zips and invisible zips can be tricky to replace: you'll need to unpick seams and, as invisible zips are often present on higher-quality garments, the lining and sometimes the hem as well to sew in a new one. Use the zipper foot on your sewing machine to get as close to the seam as possible, then carefully sew the lining closed by machine or hand.

Hola, boys!
Singlet

A LURID FUCHSIA, PURPLE AND BOTTLE-GREEN PRINT, WHICH LOOKS DIVINE AGAINST RAW SILK

I found this fabric in a flea market and snapped it up—isn't it spectacular? My bowerbird instincts drew me to the lurid fuchsia, purple and bottle-green print, which looks divine against the raw silk. It has a feather-like iridescence and petrol-ish sheen. Given its eye-popping colours, the fabric's creation likely dates to some time during the sixties.

When I bought it, I used some of the silk to make a cushion for the sofa, but still had a substantial amount left. I knew the fabric was screaming out to be worn, but couldn't quite think what to do with it—a small amount seemed statement enough. I came up with this funny little top, which I've called the Hola, boys! singlet because I think it's so darned beguiling ... one can't help being noticed while wearing it.

With a cropped front and back, but flowing sides, it's super-flattering and looks wonderful when worn layered over a simple black dress or harem pants. Pair with metallic leather sandals, a floppy-brimmed hat and copious strings of beads for all-the-way hippie luxe.

Customisation

I've no patience for patterns. I simply laid a loose-fitting vest on the fabric on my kitchen floor. Leaving a seam allowance all around, and flaring the shape out a bit at the sides to add hippie charm, I chopped around the outside of my 'pattern'. The embellished panel at the front I bought complete from a beading supplier, and ironed on—*voila!*

Minxy 159 *Vintage*

WITH CLEVER ADJUSTMENTS AND THE ADDITION OF BEADING OR TRIMS, YOU CAN CHANNEL THE CHARMS OF VENERATED EUROPEAN FASHION HOUSES

Lamé Love

As a moth to the flame, I can't help but be drawn to the metallic shine of lamé. While scratchy if worn directly against the skin, or sticky if too tight (especially under the arms), there are so many ways you can add a little lamé sparkle to your everyday and feel comfortable to boot. It's one of the few man-made fibres I wear often. With clever adjustments and the addition of beading or trims, you can channel the charms of venerated European fashion houses Chanel, Balmain and Versace.

This top from the sixties is a prime example of an old-school, high-end vintage separate now readily available in vintage stores. I bought it from a flea market for a couple of dollars, and have owned at least five or six other lamé items—all variations on the theme—over the years.

The trick to working lamé during the day is to stick to one piece as the main feature of your outfit, and pair it with simple, classic pieces; try a pair of pleat-legged pants, a sombre chignon, pearl earrings, patent flats and a knock-off 2.55 (or, if you're lucky, the real thing). But if you're out for the evening and want to make an entrance, there's no reason you can't match it with more bling in the form of metallic shoes, clutch and jewellery. You might be mistaken for a Christmas bauble, but who cares? At least you'll look game for a party. Just don't develop a last-minute attack of the shrinking violets. Wallflowers and lamé are like oil and water.

CUSTOMISATION

This gold lamé top had a moth-eaten lining which virtually disintegrated at the touch, so I snipped it away with a small pair of scissors, very close to the seams, and left the scratchy side exposed. At the time, I imagined patiently lining it with thin silk, but instead just wear it over a very thin merino wool top to protect the skin without adding bulk.

I purchased the shiny strip of discs and metallic chain-stitching on a very fine layer of tulle from specialist fabric suppliers. The embellishment cost more than the top, but it was worth every cent: I simply attached it with pins to the neckline and stitched it in place with a gold thread.

And, as much as I like boxy sixties mod-styling on others, it doesn't suit my figure, so I took this in at the sides to give it a fitted feel.

Sixties Special

When I had the figure for it (that is, when I was a beanpole teenager with no breasts or hips), I totally worked the mod look. I watched *Quadrophenia* at a local cinema, studying it as though it were a fashion spread in a magazine, and returned again for the sole purpose of taking in the distinctive styles of the mod movement. Around the same time, I started listening to The Who, The Small Faces and ska music, immediately adopting the fake lashes with heavy eyeshadow, A-line frocks and cropped hairstyles of the era—even the steel-toe-capped Doc Martens shoes with roll-cuff jeans for tomboy days. English model Twiggy was my icon, along with the designer style of Mary Quant.

My devotion to working the look ended almost overnight with the arrival of womanly curves, but an appreciation of sixties rock, ska and reggae still remains. The sheer manic energy of the music is utterly infectious and compelling; I could never grow bored of it.

This hot pink faux-organza thing is a nod to mod: I love the boxy shape paired with high collar and pleated frills. The see-through style stops it from being too frumpy, and it's totally glam paired with a sexy lace bra. All I need is a good cropped wig for the night. Work those lashes, sister.

Tip: Stained when I found it, I've worked hard to remove marks from this blouse with tea-tree oil and nappy cleaning solution, applying both by hand before soaking and hanging out in direct sunlight without rinsing. Once dry, I popped it in the washing machine for a proper rinse, on the delicate setting. When it dried for the second time, all the marks had disappeared.

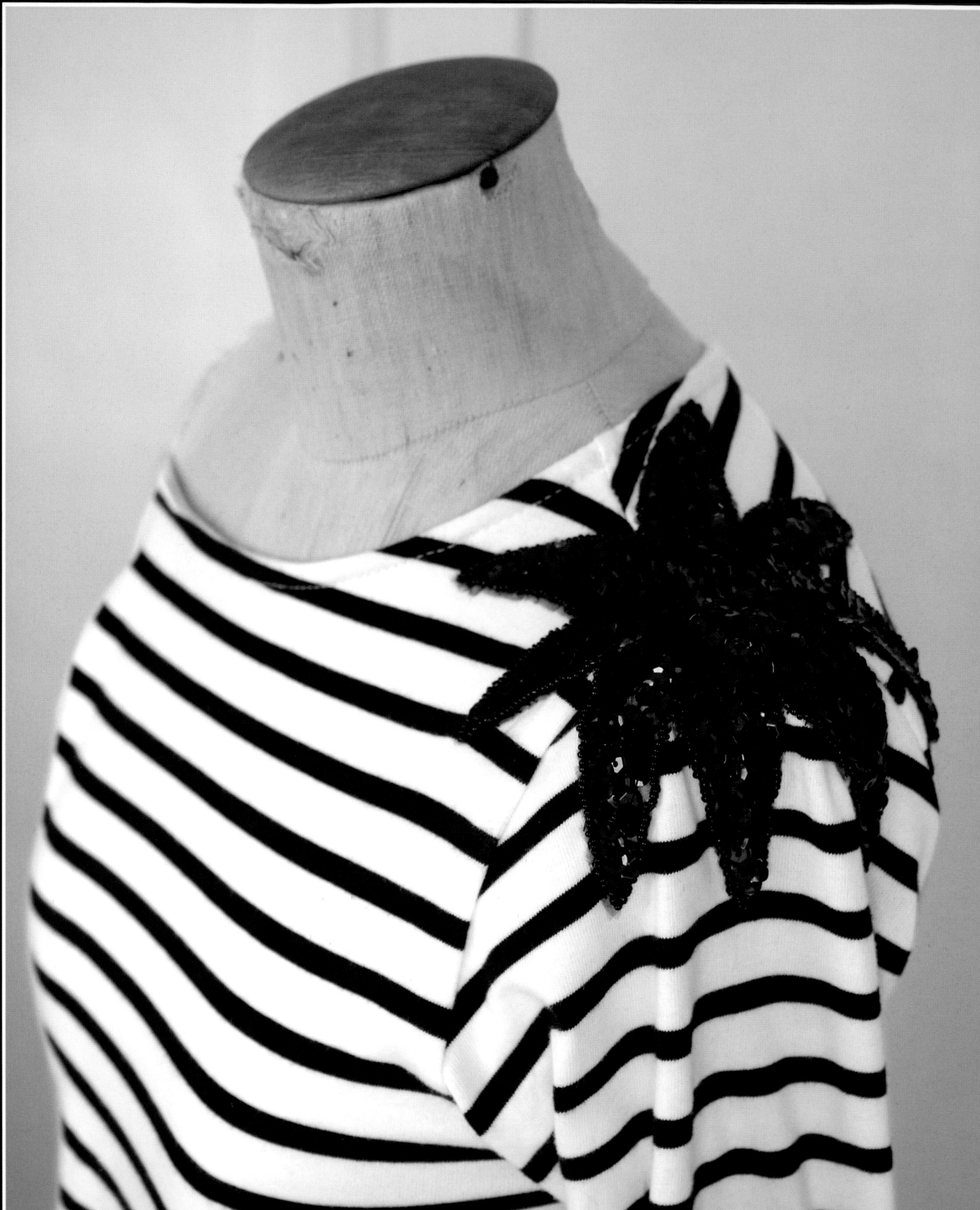

I'm no sailor
Stripe

Ever since Coco Chanel immortalised the humble Breton top with a pair of sweeping palazzo pants in 1930s France, striped tops have become a wardrobe staple for women the world over, and a kind of visual shorthand for classic cool. But while the true Breton takes its cue from sailors and other seafaring types, there are countless ways to subvert its understated simplicity by adding a little cheek or glamour. I admit I get bored wearing the basics day in, day out. Give me layered textures, floral prints, beading and sequins to pair with my stripes!

My search for the perfect Breton top took decades. Dabbling in countless imitations, I kept returning to the shapeless, boat-necked version with a background the exact shade of clotted cream, as worn by Pablo Picasso and Chanel herself. And finally, I found it in an inexpensive chainstore in Paris, adorned with a faintly naval-looking patch on the arm (which I promptly unpicked and disposed of). The beauty is, these tops are everywhere, so you should be able to find one to suit your own style and tastes. The sequinned starfish I've sewn to the shoulder was kicking about at home in a tin of bright, shiny things I'd been saving for years. I considered adding one to the other shoulder, but decided that I quite liked the asymmetric quality of it draped over one side only.

CUSTOMISING BRETON TOPS

- Sew in shoulder pads for a more commanding, stronger silhouette.
- Buy a square of plain red, black or blue cotton and cut out a bow, circle or star—even a letter, such as your initial. Appliqué it to the front, dead centre.
- Hunt down dainty floral-printed fabric and cut out the shape of a peace sign. Again, appliqué it to the front, then add vintage gilt buttons or sequins for kooky allure.
- Add contrasting pockets to the left breast, right hip or both.
- Stitch sequins across the striped lines.
- Attach gold buttons or epaulettes to the shoulders.
- Sew your top to a plain black skirt to create a simple Breton frock. This looks particularly fab when using a striped singlet and pouffy black tulle skirt. I call the look 'Ballet Breton'.
- Distress your Breton with a hundred tiny holes. Create by pinching the fabric between the fingers and nicking it with a small pair of scissors all over. Throw it in the wash, then watch the holes ladder with deliberately dishevelled charm.

White tulle ball gown, with beaded bodice and red tulle cummerbund.

Suzy Perette (a collectible 1950s label) red, black and white raw-silk party dress with original metal zipper. The hat is a 'cartwheel' style typical of the Dior New Look era, and the epitome of elegance.

CLASSIC *Fifties*

Restrictions and clothing rations finally dissipated with the post-war optimism of the 1950s, and film style once again became an overwhelming cultural influence, with screen sirens Marilyn Monroe, Grace Kelly, Kim Novak and Elizabeth Taylor all epitomising the polished elegance so many women aspired to.

Dresses were typically elaborate, feminine, princessy affairs, featuring fitted strapless bodices with nipped waists and full skirts worn below the knee. Tulle, heavy satin and lace were common fabrics for evening attire, along with tulle or nylon petticoats to lend dresses drama and fullness. They were worn with long matching satin gloves, costume jewellery and a roller-set 'do.

As the fifties wore on, the rise of rock 'n' roll culture influenced fashion, with tight-fitting sweaters, pencil skirts, pedal-pushers and voluminous circle skirts taking on sexier shapes and therefore shifting connotations, mirroring the liberation of women in post-war times. Squeaky clean Doris Day may have been the poster-girl for parents of the 1950s generation, but Elvis Presley (and his legion of female fans) was her antithesis: a new breed was forming to reject the conservatism and wartime austerity of the thirties and forties, with teens of this generation the forerunners for the feminist movement and sexual liberation of the sixties. Just watch Grease for crib notes on the shifting mores of the era, if only to enjoy watching swivel-hipped John Travolta woo Olivia Newton-John's prim Sandy.

WORK THE LOOK

The trick is to think laterally with fifties frocks: although women were generally smaller back then, there are still many larger dresses floating about which you can tailor to fit. Not all women were tiny, even if they aspired to the New Look introduced by Christian Dior in 1947, which heralded such an emphasis upon the waist.

The full-skirted fifties silhouette is enjoying such a renaissance, I would leave the style itself alone, apart from removing any unnecessary embellishment in the form of tattered silk corsages, tulle shoulder covers and diamantés, which aren't so popular with modern gals. Look for frocks that fit you in the waist or even swamp you, and take them in. If you fall in love with one that's too small, don't despair: detach the bodice and skirt and add another panel, or have a professional seamstress do this for you. It will be worth the investment if it fits like a glove.

To craftily tailor larger styles yourself, try the item on inside-out and have a friend pin the excess fabric. If your frock has prominent bust darts and you're not big enough to fill them, pin along these first, then along the sides. (Or buy a bullet bra if you fancy working an era-appropriate pointy bust.) Shimmy out carefully, before sewing straight along the line of pins, removing as you go.

If, like me, you fancy the ballerina prettiness of tulle ball gowns but mostly find them in a sorry state, remove ruined layers of tulle and replace with matching strips bought from a haberdashery. Attach grosgrain or velvet ribbons as straps if you can't bear to bare your shoulders in all their glory, or fear you don't have the 'heft' to hold the dress up.

Hemlines were fairly demure, so you might also want to raise them to show a little more leg, and remove three-quarter-length sleeves for a more modern display of exposed flesh. Pair with a tulle petticoat for proper princess flounce.

Sweet
SKIRTS

OH, FOR THE DRAMA OF A FIFTIES FULL SKIRT WITH STIFF tulle petticoats for a waspish waist ... or cheeky ruffles for girlish allure. Calf-length cotton wraparounds say hippie chick without whispering a word, and all manner of hemp-weight ethnic skirts offer worldly charm for the woman brave enough to look beyond a simple black pencil skirt for the everyday.

I collect vintage fabrics especially for skirt-making—from chintzy floral prints to fine Liberty printed cotton, tulle and silk; from ethnic embroidery to beautiful batik. I might not have the patience for constructing a fitted dress to pattern, but skirts are so darned easy, they're the one item even the most novice seamstress can make from scratch (try copying one you already have). A bit of skirt also allows for a flight of fancy without having to work a head-to-toe 'look'. But secondhand frocks and skirts often have all the material you need for customising your own style without reinventing the (cart) wheel, so look to vintage pieces first.

Denim also offers many fine opportunities. Old jeans are so readily available, you can easily set to chop-chopping them without the guilt factor. Mine your own wardrobe first or simply separate a bodice and skirt from a pretty frock. Or look to a local charity store, and find somebody to love ...

Work in PROGRESS

Add lovely ribbon loops inside a waistband to help with hanging, or employ ribbons as pretty embellishment and drawstrings.

This chintzy '50s number was way too small, and seriously stained and torn.

Collect cute or striking buttons from all manner of places and add for charming detail.

Iron-on bonding: invaluable for tear-repair and stabilising shattered silk or flimsy fabrics. Use to apply appliqué when all else fails.

Always consider salvaging skirts from ruined bodices and vice versa.

Leopard
Dreaming

Okay, so perhaps she's not such a sweet skirt (grrr) but who's splitting the difference?

You can't have a book about vintage clothing without working at least one animal print into the mix. Leopard print, specifically, is a print that never dates, evidenced by the fact it prowls through almost every season by designers good and great. They're always dreaming up new spins on an old theme. Dolce & Gabbana know that when you're on to a good thing, you stick to it, and these big cat spots have particular staying power.

Not normally fond of the carnivorous look, I love to weave a little leopard magic once in a while, in the form of a scarf or Capri pants. It's a print that looks great with all-black accessories and dull gold, but cream and beige also temper its wily temptress ways. Ditto for a splash of red in the form of a bold lip, clutch or nails … even a skinny waist-cinching belt.

This is the best leopard print item I've found: a 1980s Perri Cutten rayon pencil skirt with knock-out fishtail. Whatever you do, don't run: you might just be devoured.

CUSTOMISATION

When I tried this skirt on, it was too tight and in danger of ripping at the seams. It was also sticky-icky to wear with the original acrylic lining. I worked out that the lining was more responsible for cramping my style than the actual skirt was, so snipped it out pronto. The skirt is a lot more forgiving, and now I wear it with a silk petticoat and simple black tank.

Tip: *Sometimes fabric survives just fine and dandy while the seams themselves degrade. Natural fibres are the first to go, often crumbling in the hands with a dusty 'pouf'—especially those from the sixties and earlier. Once seams start coming apart, it's best to go over all of them on your machine to strengthen and lengthen the life of a piece; use 100 per cent polyester or poly-mix thread. I've saved many a frock from tearing open at a crucial point mid-party with this sort of early groundwork.*

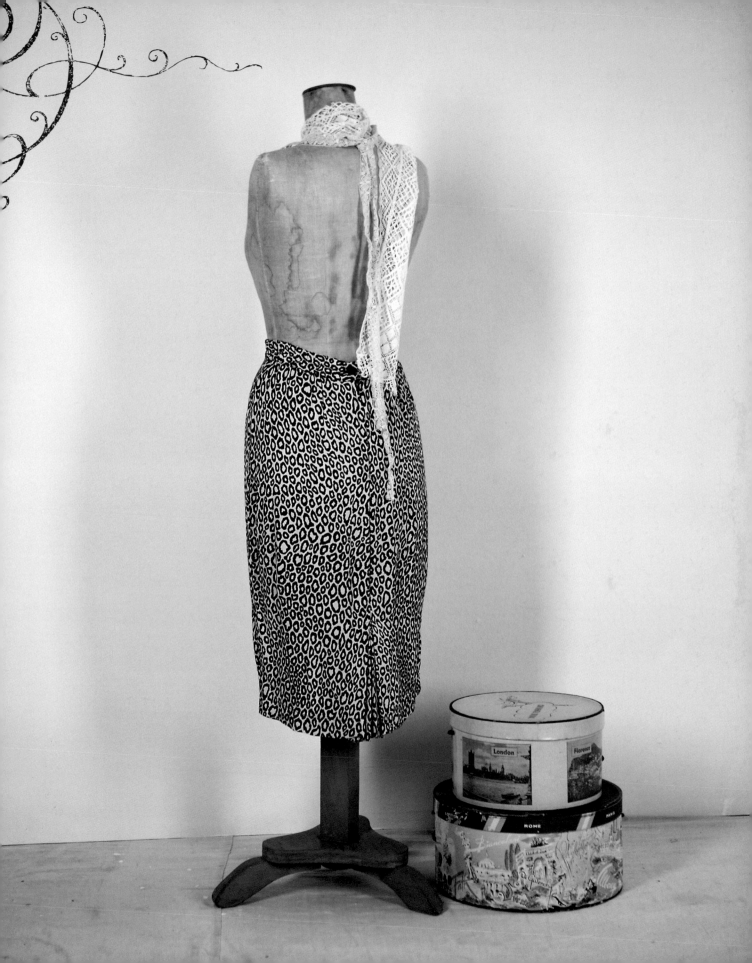

Minxy 176 Vintage

Throw him a wink
Ruffle Skirt

A cheeky red skirt feels flirty, fabulous and a *oui* bit French ... Which is why I wore this one to the opening night of the French Film Festival, the year Marion Cotillard starred in the excellent Edith Piaf biopic *La Vie en Rose*. I might have gone a bit overboard that night with the beret, and I learned my lesson: this number needs a cocktail hat, not a beret, to look fabulous. Along with a towering pair of heels to show off those pins, and a clutch in gloved hands.

This skirt's made from a lovely silk-satin, and couldn't come in a better shade of red. But she started life as a frock. Originally backless, with a high ruffle neck, I wore her once to a fancy book launch, but decided the style wasn't for me. She's so over-the-top as a skirt, I let her shine by pairing her with a basic top instead.

Customisation

The day after her literary debut, I decided to snip off the top of the dress, but realised this would leave me with half a zip. I unpicked the (invisible) zip from the top before cutting the dress, making sure the zip was opened to the bottom first. Then I cut the top off the zip, sparing a good inch or two before folding the sides under and stitching in place on the inside of the skirt. I rolled the raw edges of the snipped top part of the skirt under, and sewed it flat by hand with small, firm stitches, ironing my work into a flat band along the entire inside diameter of the skirt when done.

Tip: Whenever you see a dress you fancy for its top or skirt but not both, think about separating it. It's often easy to replace zips or find a way to use the existing one, and you can always have it inserted professionally if you're a bit scared about doing it yourself—usually at a local dry-cleaner for a tiny amount.

Tip: If you want to keep both the top and skirt of a fitted dress, add a band of grosgrain ribbon to the top of the skirt to lengthen it by an inch or so, and cover up the raw edge. If your frock's loose-fitting, create an elasticated waist by rolling over the raw edge and making a space to thread some elastic through (insert a safety pin at the end of your elastic for threading, and secure the elastic with stitches in a side seam).

Blooming belle Circle Skirt

When applied in small doses, chintz can be so gorgeous—this skirt is a case in point. I love the faded wash of colour over the fabric's rosy print, which puts me in mind of English bed & breakfasts, of being cosied up under a feather duvet with a tray of tea and toast on my lap—perhaps with a view of waves washing up against rocks in a seaside town …

This delicate silk piece was once a full-skirted frock made sometime in the early fifties. I found it in a flea market covered in tea-like stains, moth holes and with—sadly—a bodice that had been ripped to shreds. But it was far too small for me, anyway. This is how I reinvented it, brought it back to life, and made it fit.

CUSTOMISATION AND RESTORATION

My first step was to soak the silk in nappy cleaning solution overnight to diminish the stains. It worked, but the colour of the roses ran and made the rest of the fabric appear pink. I love this look—the fading and wishy-washy colour is part of its charm.

Next, I detached the bodice from the skirt by cutting across it, but I left the gathering in place. I also removed the original metal zipper completely, as it was coming away from the seams. Unpicking the too-long hem, I resewed it by hand after taking it up by a couple of inches. Before doing so, I ironed it flat so I knew exactly where to stitch.

The worst moth hole damage in the skirt was mainly located down one panel, from top to bottom. With wrong sides facing each other, I folded the moth damage over on itself and sewed down the entire length of the skirt, before chopping off the leftover fabric (eradicating the most badly affected fabric). I then folded over the seam I had just sewn, and sewed along the other side to prevent fraying (creating a French seam). From the snipped-off fabric, I cut out small pieces to cover the remaining moth holes, and applied them to the skirt with iron-on bonding.

Trying the skirt on over my head, I found she was still too small and gaped at the side where the zipper had been. Very gently, I ripped apart some of the stitching in the gathered top seam, to widen the waist, and tried it on every so often until reaching the desired width.

To create a new waistband, I cut a long strip of red cotton, folded it in half and ironed it flat. I then folded each raw edge under to meet the ironed crease.

Taking the still-gathered skirt, I pinned the cotton strip in place before machine-sewing along the bottom of the waistband to secure the skirt, removing pins as I went. I then added a button, created a buttonhole by snipping the fabric and embroidering small, firm stitches around the edges, and sewed the zipper back in place after chopping it in half.

Tip: Re-purpose original metal zippers and buttons whenever you can, if they're in decent condition. This gives the item a more authentic look and feel. To totally modernise, use nylon zippers and new buttons instead.

The button on this skirt (unseen) is vintage, taken from another item. Source vintage buttons, beads and other bits and bobs from charity stores and flea markets, even removing them from otherwise-ruined pieces. Collect a stash for future sewing projects—they really come in handy.

Bad Skirt
Comes Good

I FELL IN LOVE WITH THE EXQUISITE RAW SILK IN STRIPES OF TURQUOISE, EMERALD, SAPPHIRE AND AMETHYST

When I found this little beauty, all I could think was, *Where've you been all my life?* I fell in love with the raw silk in stripes of turquoise, emerald, sapphire and amethyst, which looks dear when paired with a pastel silk blouse and ballet flats by day, or slick with simple black and indigo accessories by night. And she's magic with a fifties tulle petticoat and towering heels—get ready for a thrilling night on the town in a flirty skirt such as this.

I only say 'bad skirt comes good' because, when found, she was far too large and frumpy. Wide in the waist, she also fell unflatteringly to the knees. She needed to go on a diet.

This skirt is one of many I've given a similar treatment to. Look out for 'bad' eighties skirts in particular: voluminous mid-calf skirts in disco fabrics abound, and languish in secondhand stores everywhere. But with a little customisation, they're ready for another spin on the dance floor.

CUSTOMISATION

Unpicking half of the waistband seam from the gathered skirt fabric (at the back), I chopped off several inches of waistband and patiently removed all the unpicked threads from both the band and skirt. Then I used my sewing machine to reattach the skirt to the shortened waistband, gathering evenly as I went, and leaving a couple of inches at the back for the clasp to connect with its other half.

I removed the waist clasp from the discarded fabric (one half of a hook-and-eye affair) and reattached it to the waistband, so that it perfectly hugs my waist when done up.

Lastly, I tried on the skirt and decided on the new length, marking with a pin. I folded over the hemline, ironed it flat, and sewed the new hem into place by hand.

Tip: *If you gather the extra fabric from an originally much-wider skirt at the back, it usually goes unnoticed or adds a little extra oomph, which can be flirty and fun. But if your skirt's really wide, you might want to detach the entire waistband and start gathering again.*

GIVE HER A TWIRL AND
YOU'LL SEE SHE'S A BLACK
MAGIC WOMAN INDEED

Disco Gypsy
Peasant Skirt

Nothing says hippie chick more than a long, loose peasant skirt. Or perhaps a peace sign or two.

I call this one Disco Gypsy because she's a bit fancy with her lamé threads and black chiffon base, and is more than capable of dancing up a storm. Give her a twirl and you'll see she's a Black Magic Woman indeed.

RESTORATION

This skirt was badly torn when I found it, and the elastic in the waist had disintegrated. I hid a large tear midway down the side of the skirt by folding over the fabric and making a thinner panel. I also made a small incision in the waistband, pulled out the elastic and rethreaded it, before machine-sewing the elastic ends together and sewing the incision closed with small, firm stitches.

Pale blue and silver geometric shift dress, typical of the mid sixties. Short in length with a nylon zipper, the all-over pattern is loud and adventurous. This would have been paired with lamé shoes and wild blue eyeshadow.

Pink psychedelic-print shift dress with nylon zipper and empire bust. The print is wild, vivid and clashing; typical of the 1960s.

CLASSIC *Sixties*

The epicentre of sixties fashion was London and its vibrant youth scene, so heavily dictated by the new, exuberant music of the era. British 'mods' defined the look of the Swinging Sixties, with sexy, bohemian French model/actress/singer Brigitte Bardot coming a close second. The younger generation embraced the mass-manufactured fashion arriving in stores weekly, and hip, beatnik looks became a fresh sensation. Clashing prints and colours—ranging from Art Deco inspiration to wild, clashing Pop Art prints—were all the rage, and the mini dress (then the 'micro mini') caused the sensation of the era with its ultra-short hemline and clean, sharp lines. Trousers became acceptable for women. Up until the sixties, trousers were seen as a poor woman's form of dress, or the sole province of working women and young girls. The look was all about the future.

Overall, sixties fashion was a riot of colour, print and style explosion, with designers Ossie Clark, Pucci, Biba and Mary Quant leading the charge. It was the era when mass-production finally took over from haute couture, which meant clothing was more affordable.

For evening, women wore either short shift-like shapes or long maxi-length dresses made from over-the-top brocades and bright colours, with make-up to match. Ensembles also became popular for evening and daywear, with jackets to match the existing dress underneath, no matter the print or colour.

Synthetic fabrics became popular in the sixties because they were easier to wear and lowered clothing costs, and brocades were a highly ornate and popular fabric for evening. The sixties was a time of exploration in fashion: plastic, vinyl, cut-outs, maxi and midi lengths and Pop Art—designers experimented with anything and everything.

WORK THE LOOK

Early sixties style is impeccable: think Audrey Hepburn in **Breakfast at Tiffany's**, or the women of 'Mad Men'. I have come to adore the shape of Wiggle dresses in particular, because they suit my tall, curvy frame, but I'm not fond of the added chiffon scarves which trailed down the back of fitted sixties evening frocks; they are too fussy and dated for my liking. Perhaps remove these and set aside for later, in case you change your mind—I'm sure I will one day, when scarves enjoy a renaissance and I suddenly need them post-haste.

Sixties lamé is super-fun for an evening look, but all that shine adds a few kilos to any frame. Tailor the sides of boxy sixties dresses and tops for a flattering, curve-hugging shape, or turn a mini into a micro-mini to leave acres of bronzed leg on display. Add a heavy dose of chunky jewellery into the mix and remove sleeves for a more party-friendly look (to dance the night away in lamé, your underarms should be left uncovered—otherwise you'll find yourself sweltering).

Remove unnecessary features such as kooky or tight necklines, outside pockets and damaged embellishment. Fill in crazy cutouts with fabric backing in a more sombre colour or print, and consider separating a top from its skirt or removing the sleeves when you find a really out-there dress which is too much for the eyes to take in—particularly maxis with stains or damage. Add internal pockets for useful chic, and glass beads to create a dramatic bodice.

For psychedelic or eye-popping floral prints in acid-brights, tone down with pastel or neutral separates, and layer under a long, modern cardi or shirt. Opt for short styles to cut down on the visual print extravaganza, or go totally over-the-top with an added marabou trim.

None-too-Nanna KNITS

FEEL THE LOVE FOR ALL THINGS WOOLLEN WHEN THE CHILL sets in, and bring dated styles bang up-to-date with a gloriously modern makeover. For the past wee while, the trend for reviving dated knits has been all the rage, so maybe it's only a matter of time before Colin Firth's reindeer number in *Bridget Jones* has its day, or Jenny Kee's loud eighties knits are so-now again … hard to say, but get dabbling for the sheer pleasure of it.

As you've no doubt gathered from the jackets and coats chapter, I don't really do 'trad' when it comes to rugging up. Knits are so soft and cosy to snuggle up in, and comfort's nothing to be scoffed at. If I can get away with wearing one and still look smart, I will, and often have a scarf at hand in the winter months (given a boring susceptibility to throat and chest infections). My current plan is to learn to knit, so I can recreate a forties bold-shouldered cardigan from a vintage pattern, inspired by the film *Never Let Me Go*.

Fashion-wise, old cardigans and jumpers allow for some fabulously odd combinations which somehow just *work*—and not only when you're young enough to pull off heavy doses of fashion irony. Mix it up, and set aside a morning in early autumn for some adventurous outfit experimentation to discover your go-to styles for the cooler months ahead.

Work in PROGRESS

hardmade with love

Tins full of embellishments dug up
in flea markets and haberdasheries add
quirky, original features to lapels and
hems. Consider having your own labels
made, and gift finds to friends.

Be astounded by the difference:
new buttons make old new again.
Don't forget your item when
choosing buttons to match.

Strips of fabric and brocade ribbons make for beautiful edging and binding of frayed hems when cut on the bias.

Bring old knits back to life with quirky embellishments. This original 1930s cardi had so many holes it took days of continuous stitching to fix, but looks almost new again with a set of lovely new buttons, canny repairs and wool thread, matched to replace various lines of pulled stitching.

Beads and sequins add glamour and drama, or simply cover up areas of damage if carefully chosen to fill missing gaps and stains.

Embroider felt flowers to lapels and over small holes.

Ever-so-lovely Jumpers

WHY WOULD YOU BUY NEW KNITS WHEN YOU CAN FIND CASHMERE FOR SUCH A STEAL?

There are so many beautiful jumpers lingering in charity stores and flea market stalls, often constructed from the finest materials (lots of nasty acrylic, too, but let that be ground up into carpet underlay—as apparently that's what happens to a significant portion of unwanted clothes). I have a theory as to why: the dated colours and styles. But as some can be acquired for less than a few dollars each, why would you buy new knits when you can find cashmere for such a steal?

Consider dyeing the base to a more fetching shade—something you'll long to wear, like fuchsia or sea-green. A colour makeover makes all the difference to boring neutrals; the knitted pieces I've decorated to my own tastes are among the favourites in my wardrobe.

But the first step for plain or damaged vintage knitwear has to be embellishment: cover holes and stains with beading, felt forms, sequins, buttons, embroidery, stitching and patches of pretty fabric and leather. Make your own bias-binding, or buy lengths made from divine floral cotton, satin or silk velvet. Make a feature of a former hole by repairing with bright wool to make a contrasting bobble, and repeat the pattern all over. The only limit is your own imagination.

BUILD A COLLECTION

For gorgeous embellishments, collect inexpensive bits and bobs whenever you find them—I'm always on the look-out for ribbons, brocades, embroidered patches of fabric, buttons, lace, buckles, bias and all manner of things. Buy high-quality wool in delicious colours, and embroidery thread for stitching shapes and letters onto fabric.

MAKE YOUR OWN BIAS-BINDING

Making your own binding is quite wasteful, as anything cut on the bias will leave a portion of unwanted fabric, but try to use as much of the length of fabric as possible. Cut strips on the diagonal, four times as wide as you want to be visible, and sew as long a strip as you require to wrap around a collar, cuff or hem. I often use chopped-up clothes in ugly styles (but gorgeous materials) for bias-binding.

When you've finished sewing your strips into one long ribbon, fold in half and iron flat. Then fold each edge in on itself and iron again. Wrap it around the edge of your item and sew into place at the appropriate spot on the outside of the fabric. Then turn inside out and sew by hand into place, threading the needle through the middle of the bias so it's invisible. This works particularly well for any item with damaged cuffs or hems, and you can make the bias as thick or as thin as you like.

Cardigan Magic

CARDIS CAN EITHER MAKE OR BREAK AN OUTFIT: JUST OPT FOR ONE THAT'S NOT TOO FRUMPY OR SHAPELESS

Cardigans get a bad rap but I'm completely obsessed with them, and wear one almost every day in the cooler months. They're such a useful item, and have the ability to either make or break an outfit: just opt for one that's not too frumpy or shapeless.

For years I've been jazzing up basics with intricately beaded vintage cardigans, shrunken bolero styles, and drapey numbers that glide over the figure while working as a wrap when the wind gets up.

I consider myself very fortunate to own not one, but two, rare finds: hand-knitted cardigans from the 1930s, in homespun designs. The reason they're so rare is because much of the knitwear from that era was unravelled during the war effort, and re-used to make blankets and socks for soldiers. It's a minor tragedy under the circumstances, but one I can't help feeling sorry about. Knits from the 1930s are simply charming, and look sweet with a 1950s-style full skirt, or modern over a tight

tee with a pair of skinny jeans, or high-waisted flares. This is my favourite—the one shown here with flower and pompom details.

HOW TO REPAIR HOLEY KNITS

Turn the item inside out. Take a needle and thread, in a slightly darker shade than your wool, and sew small stitches around the diameter of the hole. When you reach the spot where you began, pull the thread together carefully, making sure any raw edges are tucked inside, rather than outside, the garment.

If it's a huge hole, consider embellishing over it. If your knit is covered with holes too numerous to mention, you could decorate the entire thing with vintage buttons placed in a kooky pattern. For big, loopy, Aran-style knits, use a large needle and wool (rather than cotton) in a matching shade.

I own so many beaded cardis, I've lost count of how many I have floating about the house, and in my capacious repairs trunk. One of my favourites is an original creamy Pringle from the 1940s, with white beading and soft silk lining, and it's the one that cost the most: seventy dollars from an antiques fair. The rest set me back much less, which is staggering considering the amount of work that's gone into them, and the high quality of the materials. Most of the beads are fine antique glass, and the wools are either cashmere or lambswool—each is at least forty years old.

I often perform one, or all, of these actions below to my beaded cardigans, because they're charming enough not to need anything more drastic. Here are my top tips for breathing new life into old beauties.

1. Dye by hand: many vintage cardies are stained from sheer age. It's also hard to find them in some shades, such as dark pink, purple, orange or green. Common hues are pastel yellow, pink or blue, and black and ivory. Navy blue with white beading is lovely, but hard to come by—I found one once but didn't have the money to invest in it at the time. I've regretted not buying it ever since. I've dyed this cardigan lilac to the right pink; it used to be a grubby off-white (remember, colours will often finish more faded on wool and silk, which is why the lining's turned out darker).

2. Repair any gaps in beading: source new, matching beads and sequins from a haberdashery, or borrow from a less-conspicuous place on the cardigan. My pink cardigan had so many sequins missing from the lapel, bottom hem and cuffs, I completely unpicked the detailing on the lower hem and restitched sequins on obvious gaps in the lapels. This represents a significant time investment—it took at least three or four hours of continuous stitching—but I'm thrilled with the results. It now looks like a vintage cardi in impeccable condition, or a completely new designer item. It was anything but when I started.

3. Replace your lining: if the lining is ripped or the silk simply shredded—'shattered', as they say—from overuse or lack of care, replace with new fabric or a secondhand silk scarf. Lay the cardigan out on a flat surface and cut the silk to the shape of the cardi's back (from the inside), leaving a seam around the edges. Stitch in by hand.

4. Repair any holes: see the tips for repairing terribly holey knitwear (on the previous page).

5. Carefully attempt to shrink it: running your cardigan through a delicates cycle on the washing machine (inside out and fully buttoned, and inside a pillowcase to protect its beading) should be enough—just don't pull it out into shape when you're done. If your cardi is verging on small in the first place, this will give it a fitted bolero feel.

6. Replace the buttons: buttons are often missing, so try matching those remaining or replace entirely with new ones. Another option is to use deliberately mismatched buttons—this can look really great on the right item, and I've done it myself loads of times.

Tip: *Be dictated by your item and fabric when reinventing. It's hard to carry out a customisation without taking the unique cut and fall into account. Take inspiration from the design of the fabric, and consider how and where you will wear it, and what with.*

Blue seventies kaftan with gold
embroidery.

Brown and gold lamé maxi-dress;
a popular look of the disco era.

CLASSIC  Seventies

The 1970s exuded a hippie, folksy vibe, heavily influenced by the music and carefree attitudes of the time. This in turn influenced fashions of the era, with traditional craft methods such as crochet, macramé, knitting, weaving and dyeing enjoying a burst in popularity. This was all part of the self-representation and personal style of the seventies, which was partly a reaction to mass-production and the birth of the shiny disco aesthetic. Travel to far-flung places and ethnic influences were referenced by designers through embroidered kaftans, natural and embellished fabrics with mirrors and beading, fur gilets, and a recycled, eclectic look from head to toe.

Alternatives to the hippie trends were ready-to-wear lines by famous couture houses such as Yves Saint Laurent and Oscar de la Renta, who sold their lines around the world and made clothing accessible to everyone. Separates in fashion were now key components, and often replaced the dress. Yves Saint Laurent's 'Le Smoking' tuxedo suit was an identifiable look of the seventies, immortalised by the likes of Bianca Jagger. Reproduced versions made from synthetic fibres made clothing more affordable, and fabrics such as Crimplene became available and key to mass production.

The disco look evolved around the time Studio 54 became famous, resulting in luxe punk looks of lamé, patent leather and even such out-there designs as velvet bell-bottomed suits. Halston refined the look with his iconic Grecian-inspired and draped jersey dresses, which were often backless and maxi in length.

Patterns, bright prints and textures were all explored, contradicting the natural arts-and-crafts look. Designers encouraged freedom of movement in the form of kaftans, ponchos, maxi-length frocks and jumpsuits.

WORK THE LOOK

The seventies saw lots of maxi-length kaftans, frocks, skirts and jumpsuits, which are fine when made from natural fibres but not so easy to wear otherwise—particularly not in the loud prints or excessively earthy tones of the era. Remove the sleeves and shorten hemlines so your body can breathe (if you want to dabble in synthetics), or tailor particularly loose-fitting cotton or linen styles at the sides to show off your curves. Cinch kaftans with a belt at the waist or low-slung around the hips, or chop off a floor-sweeping hem for a cute smock-style mini dress. Remove high, frilled necklines and fussy cuffs to make items more wearable. Given the excessive volume of the era, seventies pieces are often greatly improved by what you take away.

Amp up folksy trends by adding embroidery in a metallic thread, or repair gaps to damaged areas of embroidery with your own. And source additional beading, injecting an evening vibe into otherwise plain pieces.

Outrageously wide, high-waisted flares were also popular in the seventies. Tone down these trousers by taking them in by a few inches down the side or inside seams, or wear with slim-fitting items on top to balance the proportions.

FOXY Accessorising

AN OUTFIT IS RARELY COMPLETE WITHOUT ACCESSORIES. This could be a simple silver pendant worn with a basic frock and bare feet; or a cocktail hat, peeptoe pumps, seamed tights and clutch bag paired with a fitted skirt suit for head-to-toe glamour. Either way, the balance needs to be right. It takes consideration in front of a full-length mirror, and a willingness to experiment, to be an accessories queen.

There are days when I've no time for proper accessorising, but I always feel more confident when I've matched a few items together. I'm not talking matchy-matchy belt, bag and shoes, or all-one-era gear. Just a good mix of stylish pieces that, when combined, create a story and set the tone for day or evening … for yourself, more than anything.

As far as I'm concerned, vintage accessories are a bargain. Particularly beaded clutches, costume brooches and cowboy boots (sadly, brooches are no longer a jewellery box staple, and although many people are squeamish about secondhand shoes, I *love* a pair of worn-in cowboy boots). But even the most popular high-end stuff can be found for a fraction of its original cost, and is worth investing in. It's certainly more valuable than standard Made-in-China fare, and often shares the same price tag (well, apart from those divine Lucite handbags, which I covet dearly, but cost a pretty penny).

For my money, stores such as Harlequin Market in Sydney's Paddington (think vintage Chanel, Lawrence Vrba and Kenneth Jay Lane jewellery, as well as a wide range of anonymous belts, scarves and bags) carry a far more interesting selection of pieces to choose from than a luxury jeweller's. And an afternoon in an antiques centre is enough to convince me that there's little need to invest in brand-new pieces.

Here are a few of my favourite ideas for reinventing, or crafting from scratch, some pieces to complete your look, and some pictures of my most treasured accessories. Give me fun costume sparklers, handmade shoes and a timeless handbag over proper jewels, any day.

Work in PROGRESS

A brace of belts: add a worldly vibe to any outfit with traditional ethnic touches.

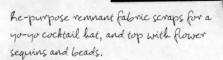

Re-purpose remnant fabric scraps for a yo-yo cocktail hat, and top with flower sequins and beads.

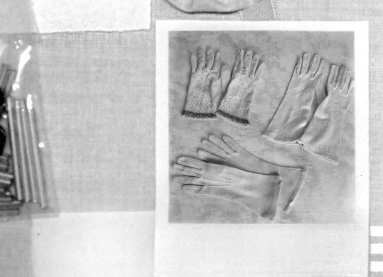

Faded, grubby gloves respond well to brightly-coloured dyes. Add a velvet ribbon bow for first-lady chic.

Sew simple beaded stars and hearts to leather ballet slippers or canvas flats for kooky, individual glamour.

Delicious silk and silk-velvet scraps — a little goes a long way. Personalise pretty hats and clutches. Create accessories from scratch.

Lovely lace edging works a treat on scarves, headbands and clutches. Keep it simple to avoid nanna references.

A riot of feathers for earthy charm. Put to use in small or large doses.

Don't restrict the dye to clothes — this tiny sequinned purse, previously stained and grubby, gets a night-out makeover.

Gloves
for glory-day glamour

FABULOUS ACCESSORIES YOU CAN WEAR WITHOUT FEELING TOO COSTUME-Y OR CONSPICUOUS

Unlike hats, gloves are one of those fabulous accessories you can wear without feeling too costume-y or conspicuous, which is weird because they scream serious style. I've been collecting them for years, and don't feel I need too much sartorial courage to wear them out with a swishy frock and towering pair of heels.

CUSTOMISATION

All four pairs of gloves were stained and grubby when I found them, and were white or neutral. I've dyed each pair when doing other items of clothing, and they all turned out so well. Although I mainly wear black beaded gloves, as they're so versatile and chic, I love brightly coloured gloves because they really pop—particularly with a clashing or neutral-toned frock. Wear them out in the cooler months, and hold draped in one hand, cocktail in the other, when you reach your destination.

Work out what your gloves need to match that perfect outfit. A new shade? A ribbon bow? Beading? Darning here and there? Be inventive.

THIS HIGHLY ADAPTABLE CLUTCH WORKS PERFECTLY FOR ALL SORTS OF OCCASIONS

Dawn-to-midnight Clutch

A clutch is so darned useful, and really polishes off an outfit—day or night. I collect beaded beauties from the Victorian era through to the seventies, and love presenting them to friends as a gift. They fit snugly in the palm or under the arm, and hold all the essentials.

Don't be put off by slight damage: many of the versions I buy are missing beads and have ripped or stained linings. I match the beads at a haberdashery store and repair by hand, replacing the silk lining with remnants from home. Damage often means they're a steal, and sometimes cost as little as a few dollars each.

MAKE YOUR OWN

Ditch your large work-style handbag and transform a daytime outfit by making this elegant reversible clutch from scratch. Cash, cards, keys, lipstick and phone should all fit comfortably into this adaptable clutch, which works perfectly for all sorts of occasions.

Be bold when choosing your fabrics: go for a sweet print for day (such as this delicate floral print), and velvet or raw silk for a luxe evening look. Add a lovely large button or two for a slick finish.

You will need:

- two rectangles of fabric, each 43 x 32 centimetres: cotton is recommended for the 'day' side, and velvet or raw silk for the evening
- optional interfacing measuring 43 x 32 centimetres: if both your fabrics are very thin, you might want to use interfacing to make your clutch's shape more defined
- two large buttons
- ruler
- scissors
- dressmaker's chalk
- needle and thread
- pins
- sewing machine and thread
- iron.

INSTRUCTIONS

1. Measure up: carefully measure and cut two pieces of fabric measuring 43 x 32 centimetres with your dressmaker's chalk, ruler and scissors.

2. Go with the curve: lay your two rectangles of fabric together, with right sides facing each other. Use a dinner plate to trace a curved edge onto the two top (long edge) corners, then trim along your traced curve—this will be the flap.

3. Attach those buttons: take your outer bag piece and, with the right side facing you, measure about 5 centimetres in from the centre top edge of the flap. Sew on your button with needle and thread, and then repeat this step for the inner bag piece.

4. Get pinning: lay your bag pieces back together, with right sides facing each other and edges aligned. Pin together. If you are adding interfacing, place your rectangle of stiff interfacing fabric on the outside and pin all three pieces together.

5. Sew it up: allowing a 1 centimetre seam, sew around the outer edges, removing the pins as you go and leaving a 10 centimetre opening in the middle of the shorter straight edge.

6. Pressed to perfection: trim away the seam allowance, diagonally, on the corners (if they're a little bulky), taking care not to cut your stitching, and then turn your clutch right-side out to press thoroughly with your iron. Turn under the raw edges on each side of the opening and press these as well—it should make your next step easier.

7. Close the deal: stitch together the short end of the bag, near the edge, with needle and thread. This will close your opening at the same time.

8. Fold the envelope: lay the bag on a flat surface with the lining facing upwards and the flap at the top. Measure up 15 centimetres on each side, from the bottom straight edge, and mark with a pin. Fold up the bottom edge of the bag at this 15 centimetre mark, bringing wrong sides together, and pin together at the sides—it should look like an envelope.

9. Sew cute: topstitch the side edges of the bag together, allowing a little velvet to show through. Start at one bottom edge and sew up the side, about 3 millimetres in from the edge, reversing a couple of times for reinforcement when you get to the opening edge. Repeat this step on the other side of the bag to complete the entire project. You're ready to hit the town.

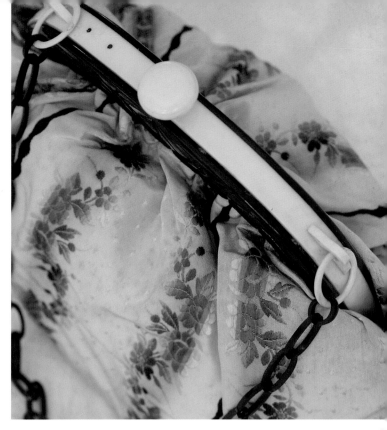

This scarf is more for daytime wear, but richly textured fabrics such as velvet, slub silk and brocade work their magic in the evening.

Toile Romance
Patchwork Scarf

I can't help hoarding pretty pieces of fabric. I have an entire cupboard full of materials I bought without a specific purpose in mind, just because I fell in love with the print or the colour or its texture. In the interests of de-cluttering I've tried to stop, but when I find something really special I'm unable to resist … a metre here and there of shop-bought lengths, chopped-up items of clothing I've saved for the material alone, and numerous scraps of ribbon and broderie anglaise and cross-stitched tablecloths. Even old flags, handkerchiefs and ties; not to mention items I've been given by friends who thought I might find a use for them.

This is patchworking in the truest sense of the tradition. Of course, there are endless new fabrics to buy: designers put out whole ranges for the specific purpose of mixing and matching. But I prefer to use up pieces of material that would otherwise go to waste, opting for my own imagination, adding bits that have sentimental value (such as the scraps from clothing I wore until threadbare) and a bowerbird find or two. That way, when I look at the patchwork I see something old and something new … all the stories behind the piece, and the layers of history it represents.

In this scarf alone is the material from a beloved pair of pyjama pants (I wore them for almost a decade), the last piece left from a lovely fabric my friend brought back from India, a scrap of 1930s sun dress, a strip of daisy embroidery I picked up in a Burgundy *brocante* on last year's trip to France, a favourite floral print salvaged from a flea market skirt, and some newly bought toile de jouy fabric from a remnant bin. I borrowed the idea from a pretty French scarf I saw which was made from vintage fabrics, but it morphed into something unique through the design I chose and my way of putting it together. For this reason, it also makes a priceless gift for a friend.

You can just imagine the mixture of emotions it conjures when I wind it around my neck.

HOW TO MAKE A PATCHWORK SCARF

Decide upon the size. I took a pashmina I wear often and love, and started layering pieces of fabric all over it, cutting to fit. When I liked the way all the pieces looked together, I started stitching them together in increments. I don't have an overlocker, so to avoid raw edges and possible fraying, I sewed each piece together with French seams. If I had an overlocker, I could have finished it in a fraction of the time—even so, it only took an hour to complete. I then added some pretty embroidered linen and cotton lace to the edges.

Twinkle Toes
Ballet Slippers

I'll share a little secret of mine: when I'm feeling overweight or uninspired, I dress in neutral shades and gorge on the accessories instead. I'll cook up new ways to use old jewellery, footwear and bags, pinning brooches or embellishment on things, and turning a necklace into a loopy bangle or bag chain for a change. I like to look at my collection with fresh eyes.

It's good to give your accessories the once-over every few months. We often forget we own things, and it can be years between wears as we opt for same-old items.

And who says customisation need be limited to your clothes? Embellish plain shoes with fake flowers, buttons, ribbons, beading and pre-made sequinned decoration, as I've done here. It's a great way to spruce up scuffed shoes, and is easily undone if you get bored of the look.

CUSTOMISATION

I'm a big fan of these lovely beaded and sequinned hearts, which you can buy pre-made. For years I've been adding lace and beads and ribbons to soft leather or cloth ballet flats (my favourite footwear), but this is by far the easiest addition: simply use an embroidery needle to stitch by hand around the outside of your chosen embellishment.

THERE'S SOMETHING SO RELAXED
AND CHARMING ABOUT CLOTH BELTS
WORN WITH A NEUTRAL FROCK OR
WILDLY CLASHING PRINTS

Curiouser and curiouser
Cloth Belts

I quite fancy a cloth belt, which is less serious and more eccentric than the leather kind—anything from traditional Japanese obis to seventies braided numbers, eighties coloured elastic or simple ribbon, and those ethnic Indian versions boasting heavy embroidery and inset with little mirrors. There's something so relaxed and charming about one worn with a neutral frock, or even wildly clashing prints.

This antique, original embroidered and mirror-inset belt from India was so long when I found it, it could only be worn around the hips. I decided to make it shorter for a waisted version, because I so rarely wear hipster styles anymore.

HOW TO SHORTEN A TRADITIONAL CLOTH BELT

Find the exact length you want your belt to be by placing it around your waist and marking the cutting spot with a pin. Cut off the excess. Embroider the raw edge, matching the authentic sewing style stitch for stitch. Reattach any ribbons or tying braid, as I've done here. You can barely tell where I've been as I copied the finish of the original belt so fastidiously.

Here's another cloth belt I've fashioned from the remnant silk I lopped off my once-long, pink silk kimono. I'd been saving this buckle for years and years, and am thrilled to have finally put it to use. It looks magic over a floaty silk frock or billowing blouse.

HOW TO FASHION A CLOTH BELT FROM SCRATCH

Use a dressmaker's measuring tape to calculate the thinnest part of your trunk. Take a long strip of fabric, and measure an extra 17 centimetres on top of your measurements (ten for extra width, five for folding over the buckle, and two for the inside seams). Cut it double the height you want the finished version to be, plus a couple of extra centimetres. This makes for a belt with little excess fabric—although you can always add more width if you want to keep your options open for a hipster belt—yet gives you some breathing space to loosen the notches after an indulgent meal.

Fold your fabric so the right sides are facing together, and sew around three edges, leaving one of the shorter edges open. Turn inside out, and roll under the open raw edges before sewing together on your machine.

Take your buckle and thread onto the fabric; fold the end of the fabric over the buckle bar and sew it flat by hand or on the machine.

Mark the spot you'd like the holes to be, 2½ centimetres apart. Use a small pair of scissors to cut the fabric, and embroider around the raw edges of the holes by hand, in a matching thread.

Exotic bird
Feathered Headdresses

Feathers are the perfect way to add high drama or hippie charm to an outfit. Think parties at home or concoct an occasion purely for the excuse to wear them. Summer bonfire, anyone? I'll wear feathers to make toast of a morning (why not?).

I love these glossy black quills, which have a luscious, deep-emerald sheen, but feel free to opt for brighter colours.

Here are two Indian-style headdresses—one squaw in style, the other the full chief—which were inspired by a picture I saw of Marlene Dietrich decked out in a bird-feather headdress.

HOW TO CONSTRUCT A SQUAW HEADBAND

Detach two or three feathers from a strip and take one length of grosgrain ribbon, along with some pretty glass beads (these came from a broken bracelet but you can use anything; earrings that have lost their partners are particularly good for deconstructing). Stitch the feathers and beads to the centre of the ribbon, by hand. Tie around your head. Eat toast.

HOW TO CONSTRUCT A HEADDRESS FIT FOR A CHIEF

Take your strips of feathers and hold across your forehead to work out how wide they should be. Cut to the correct length. Follow the same step with your strip of studs or embellishment. Iron the studs to the grosgrain ribbon (if they have an iron-on strip), or stitch together by hand. Iron on a strip of bonding to the back of your grosgrain ribbon (following the instructions on the packet) and remove the protective paper. Iron on your strip of feathers, through the strip of ribbon holding the feathers together (be careful not to have the iron set to too high a temperature, or this could scald your ribbon). Iron on another strip of feathers in this way for a layered effect, or stitch to the first layer by hand if it's too thick to allow heat from the iron through.

You will need:

- grosgrain ribbon, enough to wrap about your head and tie in a bow
- a roll of thin, iron-on bonding to iron to your ribbon
- iron
- strips of feathers, purchased from a haberdashery or over the web
- scissors
- bits of broken jewellery
- strip of studs or additional embellishment (optional)
- needle and thread.

Devil in the detail
Cocktail Hat

THE FLOWER SEQUINS AND BEADS USED HERE REMIND ME OF PRADA-STYLE EMBELLISHMENTS

I am just totally obsessed, and completely in love with, making yo-yos from vintage fabrics. I only wish they had a more sophisticated name.

Yo-yos are little circles of puffed fabric, and I use them to craft brooches, headbands and all manner of other decorative *objets*. I've experimented with making them out of all sorts of fabric weights, sizes, prints and with myriad variations on the centre decoration—to spectacular effect. I saw a woman make an entire scarf out of hundreds of tiny cotton yo-yos once, each no bigger than a thumbnail. I could never be that patient, but there are simply loads of other yo-yo projects you can perform for a quick fashion fix. They also make wonderful gifts, or pretty solo decorations if you're worried about going overboard (as I frequently do, but that's just me).

HOW TO MAKE A YO-YO COCKTAIL HAT

I bought the base of this cocktail hat from a haberdashery clearance basket after the Spring Carnival racing season. It's made of moulded straw in the shape of a half-hat, and came with the millinery elastic attached (if you can only find bases, purchase elastic separately and attach it yourself). I also collected a selection of different beads and sequins for decoration. I was particularly taken with the pretty metallic flowers, which remind me of the gorgeous frocks from Prada a few seasons ago.

Gather two or three different yet complementary fabrics. I've used a rich burgundy silk velvet, taken from a chopped-up skirt (bought at a flea market for the fabric alone—I've used it to make a clutch, a hat, a cloth bangle, and still have a quantity left over), a pink printed raw silk (taken from a too-small vintage skirt) and a remnant of Japanese cotton from a fabric shop.

Use a small plate, saucer and the rim of a wine glass as your 'patterns', tracing around the outside of each with dressmaker's chalk before cutting out your circles. For this hat, I've used three larger yo-yos, six medium-sized, and two small. To make the yo-yo itself, sew a running stitch around the outside of a fabric circle, a few millimetres in from the edge. When you reach the point where you started, pull through the thread then flatten the small, puffy bulb you are left with to create a 'flower' shape. Make a few small, firm stitches to keep your sewing in place, before decorating the centre of each with another, smaller yo-yo or sequins and beads. When all your yo-yos are complete, sew them to the half-hat.

Eat your heart out, Alice Band

To the tune of 'My Favorite Things' from *The Sound of Music*:

Pink brocade ball gowns and French beaded clutches
Satin heels and shelf busts and roses in bunches
Prim little Alice bands rich with frou bling
These are a few of my favourite things.

HOW TO MAKE A FAB HEADBAND

Hunt out boring satin-covered headbands from accessories stores. Sew or glue silk flowers, ribbons, sequins and anything else you can lay your hands on to the top for a one-of-a-kind headpiece.

I found this short length of antique embellished velvet ribbon at a flea market for fifty cents, and cut around the embroidered shapes to solve the problem of blunt edges. The headband was a dollar. Not bad for a seriously elegant addition to any up (or down) 'do.

Buckled-up Beauty

I bought this ornate vintage buckle in a French flea market, but you can pick up old buckles all over the place. Buckles are a bit like brooches at the moment: out of fashion. This means they're inexpensive and easy to find in charity stores, flea markets and haberdashery stores. They look fab when turned into jewellery or used to adorn a pair of shoes or belt.

HOW TO MAKE A BUCKLE BANGLE

Choose spriggy floral fabric for day or something glam for evening, such as raw silk or this lovely silk velvet. Cut a long, thin strip wide enough to fit the buckle in the middle when the fabric's doubled over (remember to leave a seam allowance), and long enough to wrap around your wrist and tie in a bow. Fold over, right sides together, and angle the edges diagonally, the way you would with a ribbon. Sew along three edges, leaving one of the shorter sides open. Turn inside out, then sew the opening shut by hand or on the machine, first folding the raw edges inside. Sew on the buckle, making sure it's directly in the middle, then you're done.

Tip: Apparently chokers are back ... I can't believe I'll be working a look I flogged to death in my teens, but that's fashion for you: always coming around again. Think about making a buckle into a choker by sewing it to a strip of lovely grosgrain or velvet ribbon. (You could also use this solution for your bangle, or a thin belt.)

Bewitching Brooches

I'm very fond of vintage brooches and their various styles—from animals and mythical creatures to bows and flowers, or Cubist-inspired geometric shapes and Art Deco profiles. Carved soapstone, shell and ceramic cameos also hold a special place in my heart, as well as the designs of costume jewellers Lawrence Vrba and Kenneth Jay Lane. I even love them when they have a few chips or tarnished metal, although I avoid those missing stones or pearls (the gaping holes are too sad, unless you find something to fill them). Older styles can look coolly unusual with modern clothes, and always sway your look towards the unique and original.

Although I collect vintage pieces, I also give just as many away, attaching them to cardies and dresses as gifts for friends. Damaged brooches also make for charming decoration on an elegantly wrapped gift, or can be sewn onto items if the clasp is permanently broken.

Here are a selection of some of the antique, vintage and retro brooches from my jewellery box. My current favourite is an eighties diamanté leopard, which looks particularly amazing against furs or black guipure lace.

HOW TO MAKE A REGATTA RIBBON BROOCH

Take a tie and fold the skinny end over to create a small loop. Pinch this loop between your fingers, as you continue creating loops with the length of the tie. Keep doing this, angling the loops to achieve a star-shape composed of six or eight loops. Pin the loops, then sew into place (making sure you sew through all the layers). Chop off the excess fabric at the wider end. Sew a large safety pin or brooch clasp at the back, and decorate over the stitches at the front with a fab vintage brooch, button or buckle.

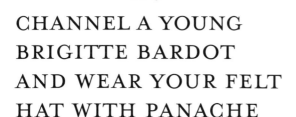

Felt love Hat

CHANNEL A YOUNG BRIGITTE BARDOT AND WEAR YOUR FELT HAT WITH PANACHE

Street-style snapper and blogger Garance Doré had the most beautiful image on her blog titled 'Ilaria Walking', which showed a willowy, Italianate brunette wearing a simple brown felt hat and camel-coloured cashmere coat.

When I saw that photo, it sent me burrowing into my wardrobe to find a brown felt hat I'd bought at the markets months before, but had neglected to wear. The problem was that my version was covered with stuck-on, tan felt flowers, which was too fussy for my liking. In the image, Ilaria's hat is adorned with a simple grosgrain ribbon. I had one of those, too, in an understated shade of French grey. Whereas Ilaria had tied her ribbon about the hat with a simple knot, I was looking for a permanent fix.

CUSTOMISATION

I set to carefully picking off the felt flowers, which had been stuck down with a glue gun. This left little bits of glue residue, which I (patiently) picked off with my nails, careful not to damage the felt any more than necessary. I then used my own glue gun to pop a few dots of glue around the base of the crown, then applied the ribbon and created a bow with the ends. Very simple, but so effective. I wear my hat to death now, channelling a young Brigitte Bardot.

Tip: *I like people who wear their hearts on their sleeves. Or their hats. Here's a too-simple idea for zhooshing up a plain beret: add a felt love heart to the front brim with some small stitches. Another idea is to add a brightly coloured pompom. Love this look—c'est tres jolie.*

Pink draped synthetic dress with competing elements typical of the era; note the draped front and back with additional side 'waterfall' drape, huge power shoulders and open keyhole at the back. This would have been worn with oversized earrings and a brightly coloured bag and shoes.

Silver and black sequinned mini dress with huge power shoulders and square keyhole back.

CLASSIC  Eighties

The 1980s was a period of oversized shapes, asymmetry, bold colours, androgyny and layering. The power suit was popular for its oversized shoulders, nipped-in waist and peplum, referencing the style of the 1940s but in a more overt way, using colour blocking to emphasise the overall effect. Power suits exerted control for the new career girls, and menswear was heavily referenced in womenswear, continuing to be influenced by Diane Keaton's style in Woody Allen's late seventies film, Annie Hall. Women wore baggy suits in houndstooth and plaid patterns, complete with ties to project a mannish, androgynous look.

Evening wear in the eighties was body conscious and avant garde, with corseted styles, short hemlines, large frills and flounces, asymmetrical shoulders, sequins and low-cut backs. It was a case of 'more is more', and dresses of the era are now considered over-the-top, with the design elements competing against each other, often in bright colours such as hot pink, sunshine yellow and lime green.

Media played a huge part in eighties fashion, with music videos and sexual imagery defining the era through bra tops, bare midriffs and asymmetry. Madonna was the iconic influence, and fashion followed the lead set by her wildly popular video clips—very few of us were immune!

Various other trends such as Victorian frills and lace, fifties full skirts and twenties-era drop-waists also made a comeback in this decade of brash excess.

WORK THE LOOK

Similar to seventies fashion, true eighties looks are usually too much when worn from head to toe. All those competing, clashing elements look more costume than clothing, and I've always found quality eighties garments can be greatly improved by taking things away. This could be an oversized bow, huge sleeves, garish faux-gem or metallic buttons, shoulder pads or lacy frills: you can usually spot them a mile off. The trick is getting the balance right: a bit of eighties flavour is great, and can look fresh when pared down.

Eighties frocks are ripe for separating into a top and skirt, and tailoring at the shoulders or sleeves. Drop waists—so fetching in slimline twenties frocks—are hideous when paired with gridiron shoulders and the excessive lace of the reinvented Victoriana trend, so epitomised by designer Laura Ashley. Take in at the sides for a flattering silhouette, and remove excessive frills and flounces. But leave the reinvented forties peplum, which is flattering to a small waist.

Most importantly, it's all about the way you wear it: if you love the over-the-top elements of a garishly embellished eighties dress, such as this black sequinned number, pair it with simple hair and make-up and toned-down accessories. Given that this dress is a mini, the only thing I'd remove is the large shoulder pads. The pink dress, however, will take much more ingenuity!

BOUDOIR BASICS & Saucy Shapewear

FOR THOSE WHO LIKE TO REFER TO A GOLDEN AGE OF SOCIETY, when ladies were (apparently) far gentler and more demure than today's women, I present you with Exhibit A: boudoir attire and shapewear from earlier eras.

Note the kinkiness of a corset. The schoolmarm strictness of a girdle. The sheer naughtiness of sheer stockings, and saucy transparent slips which glide across the female form like butter, or gently caressing hands. Garter belts and peignoirs and silk and lace teddies ... Need I say more? If you ask me, they're all sexier than today's no-nonsense G-string (even if it is more revealing), and all of them were first conceived and crafted decades, even centuries, ago to decorate the inherent beauty of the female form.

It's difficult to feel attractive in a knackered pair of knickers, or in shapeless pyjamas. Gorgeous boudoir basics are where it's at if you want to *feel* as good as you look.

Consider yourself being unwrapped like a present ... will the final reveal be the height of surprise, or a fizzing disappointment? My tip: save the granny pants for old age, and scale the heights of feminine allure while you still can.

Work in
PROGRESS

Antique nudes are
lovely in good condition.
Cover stains with dye,
or patches of pretty satin
and ribbon bows.

Replace boring straps with
vintage ribbon or lace for
striking boudoir wear.

Indulge in pretty voiles, chiffons and sheer fabrics in the bedroom or under a favourite frock.

White satin bias deals with frayed edges and hems, and stabilises flimsy fabrics.

Stitch up any tears or coming-away clasps, and dye unflattering shades a gorgeous new colour.

Grubby antique linens look so pretty with a colour makeover. The blue of Wedgewood's Delftware range is dreamiest.

Screen siren
Brassiere

A forties or fifties satin longline bra in near-new condition, which fits like a dream and makes you feel pretty enough to purr, is vintage gold dust. Snap that baby up if you ever find her.

My little beauty looks positively divine over a pencil skirt and under a cashmere cardi (forget the WASPy twinset—go the satin bra or bustier for pure sex appeal; just don't forget to leave a few pearl buttons *undone*) or on its own with a pair of silk knickers or pyjama pants. To alleviate the bullet-bust effect, line with soft cups purchased from a haberdashery.

CUSTOMISATION

If found in less-than-perfect condition, consider dyeing it to cover stains, or replacing elastic straps with silk ribbon to restore your precious find to its former glory. You can also sew in the soft cups if you don't think you'll use them with any other items.

Pretty in Pink
Petticoat

For some reason, I missed the lesson in Petticoats 101. I suspect that so too did my entire generation. It took me years to work out on my own the magically transformative effects of a decent slip or petticoat. But I have the zeal of a convert, and now possess clever vintage undergarments for almost every frock and skirt I own.

I'm always on the look-out for simple slips and pretty petticoats in soft, buttery fabrics and with varying hem lengths. They're fairly easy to find—cut on the bias for form-fitting stretch, a good slip is forgiving enough to suit a wide range of dress sizes.

I bought this pale pink silk and lace petticoat from a French *brocante*. The delicate fabric was in near-perfect condition, but it was too big—not bad for a few euros.

CUSTOMISATION

Vintage petticoats often have one piece of elastic stretched through a loop of fabric at the waist. If the elastic has disintegrated with age, or is too tight or loose to wear comfortably, it's easy to replace—which is what I've done here.

Make a small incision at one of the side seams and remove the elastic. You might need to unpick the entire loop if it's in really bad condition, and extract the 'melted' elastic from the fabric. One option is to cut off the entire waist and resew a loop to thread new elastic through, but bear in mind this will shorten the item. Pop a safety pin on one end of the elastic and thread it through by hand. Remove the pin and sew both elastic ends together by hand, before stitching the opening shut.

Tip: For petticoats and slips that are too wide, take them in with French seams at either side (to create a French seam, see Blooming Belle Circle Skirt, page 178).

Circus queen
Girdle

JUST KNOWING YOU HAVE THIS ON UNDERNEATH YOUR CLOTHING IS A DELICIOUS THRILL, AND LENDS AN INDEFINABLE AIR OF ALLURE

I love this slinky satin girdle so much, I wear it as both underwear and outerwear. It looks strange and fabulous over a frock as a sort of belt/skirt, and reminds me of the carnival atmosphere of those early Jean-Paul Gaultier perfume ads, with all the saturated colours.

Not usually one for restrictive shapewear, I throw my reservations out the window for a gorgeous girdle and proper stockings. Just knowing you have this on underneath your clothing is a delicious thrill, and lends an indefinable air of allure.

CUSTOMISATION

When I found this girdle it was badly damaged with rust stains from the metal clasps, and far too tight. I unpicked a few of the darts and boned seams for some precious extra room, then dyed it royal blue. Stitched to the side is a sequinned and beaded silver heart, which I purchased pre-made. I'm clearly thinking of that lovely trapeze artist, again.

THE FACT THEY'RE
WORN UNDERNEATH
A SKIRT OR FROCK
MEANS IT REALLY
DOESN'T MATTER IF
THEY'RE SHOWING
SIGNS OF AGE

Perfect pouf
Petticoats

I have an almost obscene number of tulle petticoats ... the legacy of a childhood ballerina fantasy, I'm afraid. My poor husband is so sick of wading his way through them in the wardrobe that I've taken to hanging them from the picture rails.

You can buy new petticoats for a proper fifties silhouette, because they're still making them, but there's really no need: there are lots of old ones available, and even if they're quite damaged, the fact they're worn underneath a skirt or frock means it really doesn't matter if they're showing signs of age.

Here is an original fifties full petticoat in red tulle, a steal from my local flea market. I gave it a quick dunk in a delicate wool wash and replaced the waistband by simply sewing over the original taffeta waistband with a longer length of grosgrain ribbon, and reattaching the hook-and-eye arrangement to fit.

The goddess sleeps
Negligee

THIS SILK TAFFETA NEGLIGEE FROM THE 1940s MAKES ME FEEL EVERY INCH THE GODDESS

In the past I admit to thinking that there was nothing sexier than throwing on a pair of boy's boxers and a well-worn, shapeless tee for bed. Times have changed. That might have looked cute on my twenty-year-old self, but I've come to the conclusion that real women either wear properly pretty things to bed, or sleep *au naturale.*

This silk taffeta negligee from the 1940s makes me feel every inch the goddess. And as you know, that's the point.

CUSTOMISATION

As you can see from the 'before' image, I've replaced the original straps with extra-wide, 1920s French ribbon—this small change has made the slip look unusual and special, and far more expensive than the few dollars it cost me to update.

The stitching in the bust darts was coming away when I found it—including at the centre of the chest. I realised this was the only reason it fit me across the bust, so continued unpicking it and created a new neckline altogether, opening up the cleavage area.

Acknowledgements

Thank you to everyone at Murdoch Books for your constant enthusiasm and talent, and for being so blessedly easy to work with. Particular thanks go to Joan Beal, Cara Codemo, Amanda Carmen Cromer, Tania Gomes, Diana Hill, Mary-Jayne House, Sophia Oravecz, Karin Pfaff, Abba Renshaw, Vivien Valk, Ashlea Wallington and Scott White for your tireless work on *Minxy Vintage*, and to the entire Australian and UK sales teams. And to Kay Scarlett, for her vision and accepting it for publication in the first place.

Mille grazie to designer Jessica Guthrie of Coco Repose, who shared her fashion history knowledge for the classics sections, wrote the foreword, and loaned so many of her museum-quality pieces to illustrate this book. I am so grateful for your friendship and thoughtful support; it's lovely having someone to witter on about fashion with at such length.

Thank you to awesome photographers Natasha Milne and Anthony Ong, as well as Iren Skaarnes, Joel Forsyth, Amanda Mahoney, Clare Thompson and Sun Studios, who worked wonders with the magic of lighting, makeup, photography and styling. You're all total rock stars — I salute you.

To the lovely Jill Jones-Evans and her team at The Victoria Room, many thanks for allowing us to shoot in your beautiful venue, and to Angela Purnell of Books & Nooks. I really appreciate your generosity and support.

Thank you to the gorgeous Kiki of The Hamper Store, for not only donating flowers, but for taking two days out of her busy schedule to act as Girl Friday on our shoot fetching ribbons, paint and all manner of other necessary items.

Thank you to Andrew, Leonie and Casey at Ici et La for providing such a gorgeous backdrop to our out-and-about shots, and for accommodating us. Thanks to Tessuti as well for allowing us to shoot in-store, and thank you to the team at Polli for your continuing support and for providing us with your striking jewellery. Sarah Wheatley and the team at Calico & Ivy Balmain were also incredibly helpful and supportive — I really appreciate all the advice and inspiration. The Sydney Antique Centre also allowed us to shoot in its wonderfully inspiring environment — thank you for hosting our book launch and exhibition.

Thanks as well to the organisers and stallholders of Rozelle Markets for fuelling my flea market obsession for almost twenty years now, and allowing us to photograph their stalls.

Thank you to my savvy agent, Jennifer Naughton of RGM, for championing me and my books, and to the divine Jonah Klein for introducing us.

Published in 2011 by Murdoch Books Pty Limited

Murdoch Books Australia
Pier 8/9
23 Hickson Road
Millers Point NSW 2000
Phone: +61 (0) 2 8220 2000
Fax: +61 (0) 2 8220 2558
www.murdochbooks.com.au
info@murdochbooks.com.au

Murdoch Books UK Limited
Erico House, 6th Floor
93–99 Upper Richmond Road
Putney, London SW15 2TG
Phone: +44 (0) 20 8785 5995
Fax: +44 (0) 20 8785 5985
www.murdochbooks.co.uk
info@murdochbooks.co.uk

For Corporate Orders & Custom Publishing contact Noel Hammond, National Business Development
Manager

Publisher: Diana Hill
Designer: Tania Gomes
Photographer: Natasha Milne and Anthony Ong
Project Editor: Sophia Oravecz
Production: Joan Beal

Text copyright © Kelly Doust 2011
The moral right of the author has been asserted.
Design copyright © Murdoch Books Pty Limited 2011
Photography copyright © Natasha Milne and Anthony Ong

All rights reserved. No part of this publication may be reproduced, stored in a retrieval system
or transmitted in any form or by any means, electronic, mechanical, photocopying, recording or otherwise,
without the prior written permission of the publisher.

National Library of Australia Cataloguing-in-Publication entry

Author: Doust, Kelly.
Title: Minxy vintage how to customise and wear vintage clothing / Kelly Doust.
ISBN: 978-1-74266-096-7 (hbk.)
Subjects: Vintage clothing.
             Clothing and dress.
Dewey Number: 646.478

A catalogue record for this book is available from the British Library.

Printed by 1010 Printing International Limited, China

Kelly Doust is the bestselling author of *The Crafty Minx*, *The Crafty Kid* and *A Life in Frocks*. She has been scouring flea markets and charity stores for vintage fashion, fabric and homewares from her early teens, and making and reinventing things in her own trial-and-error way since she was a girl. Kelly appears as a regular craft expert on television shows such as *Sunrise*, *The Morning Show* and *Mornings with Kerri-Anne*. With a career spanning book publishing, public relations and freelance writing in Sydney, Hong Kong and London, Kelly currently writes for *Vogue* and *Australian Women's Weekly*, and is working on her fifth book. Visit her blog at www.thecraftyminx.com.au.